Sous Chef

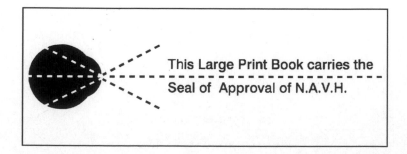

This Large Print Book carries the
Seal of Approval of N.A.V.H.

SOUS CHEF

24 HOURS ON THE LINE

MICHAEL GIBNEY

THORNDIKE PRESS

A part of Gale, Cengage Learning

GALE
CENGAGE Learning·

Farmington Hills, Mich • San Francisco • New York • Waterville, Maine
Meriden, Conn • Mason, Ohio • Chicago

GALE
CENGAGE Learning®

LIBRARY OF CONGRESS CATALOGING-IN-PUBLICATION DATA

Gibney, Michael.
    Sous chef : 24 hours on the line / by Michael Gibney. — Large print ed.
       pages cm (Thorndike press large print nonfiction)
       ISBN 978-1-4104-7150-5 (hardcover) — ISBN 1-4104-7150-0 (hardcover)
    1. Gibney, Michael. 2. Cooks—New York (State)—New York—Biography. 3.
Food service management—New York (State)—New York. 4. Kitchens—New
York (State)—New York—Management. I. Title.
    TX649.G53A3 2014b
    641.5092—dc23
    [B]   2014014456

Published in 2014 by arrangement with The Ballantine Publishing
Group, a division of Random House LLC, a Penguin Random House
Company

Printed in the United States of America
1 2 3 4 5 6 7 18 17 16 15 14

For my family

Fyodor Pavlovich, when he heard about this new quality in Smerdyakov, immediately decided that he should be a cook, and sent him to Moscow for training. He spent a few years in training, and came back much changed in appearance. He suddenly became somehow remarkably old, with wrinkles even quite disproportionate to his age, turned sallow, and began to look like a eunuch.

— FYODOR DOSTOYEVSKY,
The Brothers Karamazov

CONTENTS

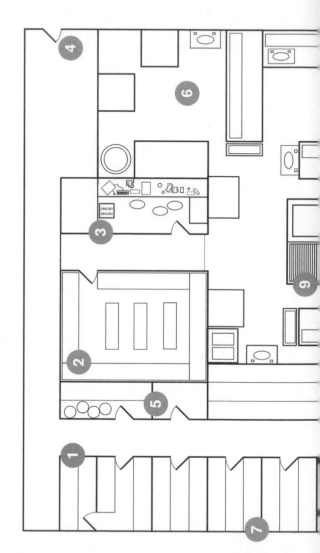

KITCHEN FLOOR PLAN

1. Walk-in Freezer 2. Locker Room 3. Chef Office 4. Exit to Loading Dock
5. Curing and Ripening Rooms 6. Pastry Department 7. Walk-in Boxes
8. Dry Storage 9. Hot Side 10. Cold Side 11. Prep Area 12. The Pass
13. Coffee Station 14. Production Storage 15. Dish Area 16. Entrance
17. Exit to Dining Room

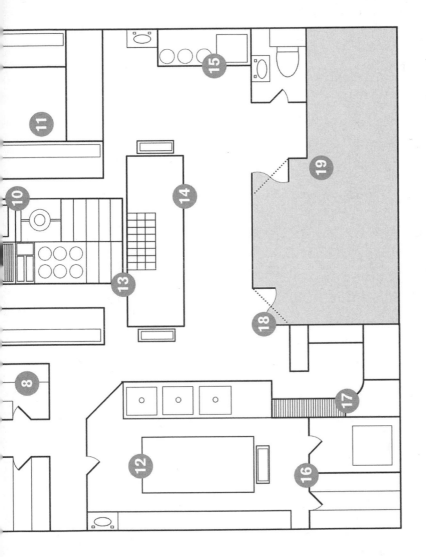

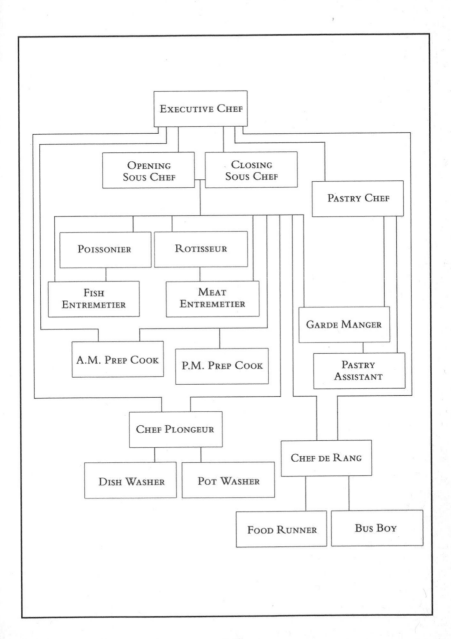

PREFACE

On a warm afternoon in the spring of 2011, I found myself on a shady corner of Forty-Third Street, just off Times Square, smoking one last cigarette before returning to the twentieth floor of the Condé Nast building to complete the second half of my day clipping magazine articles for *The New Yorker*'s editorial library — a temporary gig I'd taken between kitchen jobs. I was about to chuck the butt into the gutter when, out of the corner of my eye, I spotted a figure whose large silhouette seemed familiar enough to warrant a second look.

He was a tall man — at least six foot three — with a mange of unattended curls atop his head that made him appear even taller. He stood with his back to me, a navy-blue pin-striped suit hanging loosely over his broad shoulders. He puffed at a cigarette and chatted on his phone, making lively gestures with his free hand while a nimbus of smoke collected in the air around him.

Even though I couldn't see his face, there was something about his posture that I recognized immediately. He was poised, yet oddly stooped at the same time. His movements were quick and fitful, yet marked by a certain calculated, meditative finesse, which could be detected even in something as simple as the way he flicked the ash from his cigarette.

And then my eyes fell on his shoes and it hit me: checker-print slip-on tennies — with a suit, no less. I knew this man: Chef Marco Pierre White.

I lit up another smoke and waited for him to finish his phone conversation so I could say hello.

Of course, I didn't actually *know* the man; I only knew *of* him. I had read his books and I had seen the hoary BBC clips of him preparing *noisette d'agneau avec cervelle de veau en crépinette* for Albert Roux while a young Gordon Ramsay traipsed around in the background trying to make his bones. I knew that he was the kitchen's original "bad boy," the forerunner of our modern restaurant rock stars. I knew that he was the first British chef (and the youngest at the time — thirty-three) to earn three Michelin stars, and I knew that the culinary world quaked when he decided, at age thirty-eight, to give them all back and hang up his apron. And I knew that in recent years he'd made his way back to the stove, in one form or another, on television and elsewhere. So while I didn't *actually* know him, I did know that no matter how gauche it is to descend starstruck upon idols, I couldn't pass up the opportunity to make his acquaintance.

At first, I was met with the annoyance and reservation one comes to expect when approaching celebrities on the streets of Manhattan. I assume he thought I knew him from television. But once I announced that I was a fellow chef, and mentioned the inspiration I drew as a young cook from his books *White Heat* and *Devil in the Kitchen,* he let his guard down and we were able to speak casually. Over the course of five or ten minutes, we talked about the craft of cooking, its values and its drawbacks, and what pursuing it professionally does to the body and mind.

Eventually he had to get going, and I had to return to work as well. I concluded the conversation by asking him how he felt about quitting the industry. He paused dramatically and pulled on his smoke.

"No matter how much time you spend away from the kitchen," he said, "cooking will always keep calling you back."

We pitched our butts and parted ways.

I was sixteen years old when I started working in restaurants. I managed to land a job washing pots in an Irish pub owned by a high school friend's father. Half an hour into my first shift, the floor manager swept into the kitchen in search of a dishwasher.

"Hey, you," he said. "Some kid puked in the foyer. I need you to clean it up."

It was then that I decided I had to become a cook — if only to avoid vomit detail.

More than thirteen years have passed since I made the decision. In that time, I've seen all manner of operation — big and small, beautiful and ugly. I've climbed the ladder from dishwasher to chef and cooked all the stations in between. The experiences I've had along the way have been some of the best ever and some of the worst imaginable. What follows is my attempt to distill these experiences into a manageable, readable form: a day in the life, as I have seen it.

Within these pages, I've compiled material from several different restaurants and several different periods in time. I've also sometimes modified the names of people and places. In all instances, I've done so in service of authenticity and concision. I don't presume to offer some judgment of the restaurant business as a whole. I only hope to provide a genuine impression of the industry, to throw its nuances into sharper relief, so that when you, the aspiring cook or the master chef, the regular diner or the enthusiastic voyeur, wish to reflect on the craft of cooking, you can do so from a slightly more mindful perspective. I leave it to you to weigh the virtues and vices.

And now to work.

Morning

The kitchen is best in the morning. All the stainless glimmers. Steel pots and pans sit neatly in their places, split evenly between stations. Smallwares are filed away in bains-marie and bus tubs, stacked on Metro racks in families — pepper mills with pepper mills, ring molds with ring molds, and so forth. Columns of buffed white china run the length of the pass on shelves beneath the shiny tabletop. The floors are mopped and dry, the black carpet runners are swept and washed and realigned at right angles. Most of the equipment is turned off, most significantly the intake hoods. Without the clamor of the hoods, quietude swathes the place. The only sounds are the hum of refrigeration, the purr of proofing boxes, the occasional burble of a thermal immersion circulator. The lowboys and fridge-tops are spotless, sterile, rid of the remnants of their tenants. The garbage cans are empty. There is not a crumb anywhere. It smells of nothing.

The place might even seem abandoned if it weren't for today's prep lists dangling from the ticket racks above each station — scrawled agendas on POS strips and dupe-pad chits, which the cooks put together at the end of every dinner service. They are the relics of mayhem, wraiths of the heat. In showing us how much everyone needs to get done today, they give us a sense of what happened in here last night. The lists are long; it was busy. The handwriting is urgent, angry, exhausted.

But now everything is still.

On Fridays you get in about 0900. As you make your way through the service entrance, a cool bar of sunlight shines in from the loading dock, lighting your way down the back corridor toward the kitchen. Deliveries have begun to arrive. Basswood crates of produce lie in heaps about the entryway. A film of soil still coats the vegetables. They smell of earth. Fifty-pound bags of granulated sugar and Caputo 00 flour balance precariously on milk crates. Vacuum-packed slabs of meat bulge out of busted cardboard.

You nose around in search of a certain box. In it you find what you desire: Sicilian pistachios, argan oil, Pedro Ximenez vinegar, Brinata cheese. These are the samples you requested from the dry goods purveyor. You take hold of the box, tiptoe past the rest of the deliveries, and head to the office.

The office is a place of refuge, a nest. The lights are always dim inside. It is small, seven by ten feet maybe, but it's never stiflingly hot like the rest of the kitchen. A dusty computer, its companion printer, and a telephone occupy most of the narrow desk space, while office supplies, Post-it notes, and crusty sheaves of invoice paper take up the rest. Below the desk is a compact refrigerator designated FOR CHEF USE ONLY. It holds safe the chefs' supply of expensive perishables: rare cheese, white truffles, osetra caviar, bottarga, fine wine, sparkling water, snacks. Sometimes, there'll be beers in there; in such cases, there'll also be a cold cache of Gatorade or Pedialyte for re-upping electrolytes. Alongside the refrigerator is the all-purpose drawer, which contains pens and scratch pads, first aid kits, burn spray, ibuprofen, pink bismuth, and deodorant, as well as a generous supply of baby powder and diaper rash ointment, which help keep the chafing at bay and stave off the tinea. At the edge of the desk is the closet, overstuffed with chef whites, black slacks, aprons, clogs, and knife kits. Shelves of cookbooks adorn the walls' highest reaches, and below them hangs a mosaic of clipboards fitted with inventory sheets, order guides, BEOs, and SOPs. One of the clipboards — the one with your name on it — holds a near infinity of papers. On each sheet is a list of things to do: things to order, things to burn out, people to call, emails to send, menus to study, menus to proofread, menus to write, menus to invent. . . . You try not to look at your clipboard first thing in the morning.

As the opening sous chef, the first thing you do is check for callouts. In good restaurants, these are rare. A good cook almost never misses a shift. He takes ownership of his work; he takes pride in it. He understands how important he is to the team and he will avoid disappointing his coworkers at all costs. Regardless of runny noses or tummy trouble, regardless of stiff necks or swollen feet, regardless of headaches or toothaches or backaches, regardless of how little sleep he got the night before or what fresh hell his hangover is when he wakes up, a good cook will always show up for work in the morning. But things happen, of course, and sometimes even the most high-minded cooks must call out. And when they do, it's up to you to find someone to cover for them. Given the limited roster of cooks in most restaurants, this task is often extremely difficult — something of a Gordian knot. So, if the problem exists, it's important to diagnose it as early as possible.

If there aren't any callouts, you get a cool, peaceful moment in the shadowy office to take stock. This moment is a rare encounter with tranquillity that must be relished. You chomp on a hunk of the morning's freshly baked bread and click through your email. You fire up a few eggs over medium, trade morning text messages with your girlfriend. You duck out and smoke some cigarettes on the loading dock, step over to the corner store for a seltzer and a paper. You do as little as possible for as long as you can. For now, for just this very moment, the kitchen is yours.

Eventually your attention turns to the box of samples. It is fully within your purview — in fact it's your charge — to inspect them for quality. The executive chef has made this clear. He trusts your instincts and expects you to act on them. Nevertheless, an adolescent excitement stirs in you when you open them up.

The Sicilian pistachios, forest green, are soft in your hands, succulent in your mouth. They are rich and sweet, like no nut you've had before. You twist the cap on the argan oil and a sumptuous perfume fills the air. Drops of the golden liquid trickle down the neck of the bottle onto your knuckles. Wasting it would be a sin. You lick it off. It is robust, plump, nutty. The PX vinegar counters the sultry fat with a sharp burst of sweetness. Unlike most vinegar, this redolent nectar is thick and syrupy, with layers of flavor.

The Brinata — the queen piece, wrapped in white paper with a pink ribbon — summons you. You gently lay the cheese in the middle of the desk and begin to undress it, slowly peeling away the wrappings to reveal a semihard mound with delicate curves and moon-white skin. To use your fingers would be uncivilized. You trace the tip of a knife across the surface in search of the right place to enter. In one swift motion, you pierce the rind and thrust into its insides. You draw the blade out, plunge in again. You bring the triangle to your lips. It melts when it enters your mouth. Your palate goes prone; gooseflesh stipples your neck.

This is the life, you think.

Afterward, you smoke another cigarette out on the loading dock and ready yourself for the day.

ROUNDS

Time to get changed. You riffle through the office closet until you find a freshly pressed coat with your name on it.

Good whites are designed to be comfortable for the long haul — the hot, extended blast. Your coat, fashioned of high-thread-count cotton, buttons up around you like a bespoke suit. Unlike the standard issue line cooks' polyblend, the material for the chef's coat is gentle on the skin, with vents in the armpits to let in air when it gets hot. Your black chef pants, in contrast to the conventional, ever-inflexible "checks," are woven of lightweight, flame-retardant fabric meant to keep your bottom safe when hot grease splashes and fires flare. They slide on like pajamas. Your shoes, handmade Båstad clogs, conform to your feet like well-worn slippers. They're ergonomically designed to reduce joint and back pressure, with wooden soles lined with a special rubber that's engineered to withstand chemical erosion and to defy slippery floors. When properly dressed, you're clad in custom-fitted, heat-resistant armor that's light as a feather and comfortable as underwear.

Also in the closet is your knife kit. This kit represents everything you are as a cook and as a chef. Not only does it contain all the tools you need to perform the job, but its contents also demonstrate your level of dedication to the career. Certain items define the most basic kit: a ten- or twelve-inch chef knife, a paring knife, a boning knife. Other additions, though, might indicate to your colleagues that you take your involvement in the industry a little more seriously: fine spoons, a Y peeler, a two-step wine key, cake testers, forceps, scissors, miniature whisks, fish tweezers, fish turners, rubber spatulas, small offset spatulas, a Microplane, a timer, a probe, a ravioli cutter, a wooden spoon. . . . While these items are typically available for general use in most kitchens, having your own set shows other cooks that you are familiar with advanced techniques and that you know what you need in order to employ them. Also, having such a kit at your disposal means that you are ready to cook properly no matter what the circumstances.

Most important, though, your knives themselves tell how much the job of cooking means to you. A dull knife damages food. We are here to enhance food. Extremely sharp knives are essential for this purpose.

No one makes knives better than the Japanese. Every Japanese knife is perfectly balanced to perform a specific function, a specific cut. Its precision in this respect is unrivaled. Its sharpness, too, is unmatched. The metallurgy is most refined, a coalition of hardness and durability. No sophisticated kit lacks Japanese blades.

You take a moment in the office to examine yours, reflecting on your level of dedication. You know these knives as you know your own body. Their warm Pakkawood handles have shrunk and swelled to fit your hands; each blade welcomes your grip the way a familiar pillow welcomes the head at day's end. You could cut blind with any of them. Their individual features, their nuances, are so entrenched in your muscle memory that even as they sit on the table, you can imagine how each one feels when you hold it.

The nine-inch Yo-Deba is bulky in the hand. She is top-heavy — a bone cutter, built to cleave heads and split joints. Beside her is the seven-inch Garasuki, a triangle of thick metal, meant to lop apart backs and shanks. She's heavy, too, but more wieldy, with a weight that's balanced at the hilt. Her shape tapers sharply from a hefty heel to a nimble nose, delivering her load downward to the tip. Honesuki, Garasuki's miniature sister, sits beside her, similar in shape but lighter and more agile, for dainty work among tendons and ligaments. Even more ladylike is the Petty. Her slim six inches slither precision slits deftly through the littlest crevices. She works tender interiors, snipping viscera from connective tissue. Next to Petty is Gyutou — "Excalibur," as you like to call her. She is the workhorse of the pack, trotting her ten inches out whenever heaps of *mise en place* need working through. And at the far end, finest of all, is the slender Sujihiki. At eleven inches she's the longest of the bunch, but despite her size, she's the most refined. She's not built for the brute work of the other blades — she's made to slice smoothly. A one-sided edge optimizes her performance. While her outward lip traces lines in flesh with surgical exactitude, the convex shape of her inward face attenuates surface tension, releasing the meat. Cuts go slack at her touch; fish bows beside her.

Here they lie before you, not reflecting light but absorbing it. They don't shine like the commercial novelties on television. No, they are professionals — hand-folded virgin carbon steel. A bloomy patina colors each of them, nearly obscuring the signature of their maker. To some people, this gives the kit the tatty look of disuse. For you, it does the opposite. You see care and commitment in their dusky finish. You see a decade of daily work: a farm's worth of produce cut, whole schools of fish filleted, entire flocks of lamb broken, thousands of hungry mouths fed. You see their maker's hand in crafting them so well that they would last you this long. And you see a lifetime more in them, so long as you remain committed to keeping them clean and rust-free and razor-sharp.

Stefan, the closing sous chef, is due in shortly, and Bryan, the executive chef, won't be too far behind him. You've been here almost an hour; the real work must begin. Espresso jolts you into action.

You start by greeting anybody who might be in the kitchen. There aren't many people in at this hour — an A.M. prep cook, a baker maybe, a dishwasher or two — but you must see them and shake their hands. It's an opportunity to confirm that anybody who is supposed to be in is in, and that everybody is working on something constructive. It's also an opportunity to let them know that you are here, in case they get the idea to mess around. Moreover, it's a signal of respect. A handshake in the morning is an important mutual acknowledgment of the fact that outside our work, we are all human beings, not just cooks or chefs or dishwashers.

"*Dimelo,* baby," you say to Kiko, the senior dishwasher.

"*¿Que onda, güero?*" he says, turning from the slop sink to greet you. His hands are perpetually wet; he extends one out for the shake.

"Where's Don Rojas?" you ask. "He's here?"

"*Sí, papito, ahi atrás.*"

"*Bravo,*" you say. "*¿Todo bien contigo?*"

"*Sí, güey. Siempre.*"

You make your way to the back prep area — the production kitchen — to greet Rogelio, the A.M. prep cook. He's loading split veal shins into a fifty-gallon cauldron. His forearms are thick and rippled from decades on the steam kettles and tilt skillets. You shake his hand and leave him to his work.

After the greetings, it's time to do the

rounds. First is a walk-through of the line.

The line is the nexus of the kitchen — the main stage, where thrills reside. It's where the cooking gets done, where mise en place is transformed into meals, moment by moment, hour by hour, day by day. The three-hundred-square-foot section of the kitchen where half a dozen cooks and chefs work long into the night, straying seldom but moving much.

Our line — generously sized and uncommonly well appointed for a downtown New York restaurant with ninety seats — is set up in the traditional fashion, with Escoffier's brigade system in mind. The hot side is T-shaped, with a made-to-measure Bonnet stove as its centerpiece. This five-by-fifteen-foot gas range of Herculean capabilities is the island suite around which the cooks run their various stations. At the far corners of the range are a grill and a *plancha,* for meat and fish roasting; in the center are a row of steel-grid burners, a pasta cooker, and a fry-olator; at the near end are a pair of cast-iron flat-tops. Above the stovetop is an open-flame salamander and some pan shelving; below is a fleet of gas ovens and hot cupboards.

Perpendicular to this apparatus and forming the horizontal line of our T is the pass

— *le passage.* The pass is composed very simply of a flat, sturdy stainless-steel table, above which hangs a set of telescoping heat lamps and below which rests an assortment of clean china. It's called the pass because this is where the cooks pass their food to Chef for plating, and where Chef passes the food to the back waiters for serving. Nothing comes or goes in the kitchen without a stop at le passage.

Flanking our T on either side is a row of lowboy refrigerators, one a mirror image of the other. The lowboys hold the cooks' cold mise en place throughout service. They also act as work surfaces, upon which the cooks do their cutting and seasoning and arranging of ingredients. Above the lowboys are welded shelves that hold the sections' printers and ticket racks, along with some side materials — C-folds, gloves, bar mops, etcetera. Below the lowboys lie the black carpet runners, which keep the cooks from slipping as the tile floors get slick with this or that refuse throughout the night.

Our cold side is set up to the right of the T, beyond the fish station's lowboy. The cold side is home to *garde manger* and pastry. It's composed of a roll-in freezer, two lowboys, and a connecting table that combine to form a narrow U shape inside which two people can work comfortably. Since most of the food emanating from this section is cold, the emphasis here is on refrigeration. There is not much in the way of heat, not even a gas feed. The two stations are rigged up sparingly with two induction burners, a circulator, and an electric tabletop convection oven, nothing more.

These two areas, the hot and cold sides of the line, are central to the restaurant, both spatially and ideologically. The entire operation revolves around them. Without a kitchen there is no restaurant; without a strong line there is no kitchen. Therefore, it is essential to maintain cleanliness and order in these areas.

When they arrive in the morning, Rogelio and Kiko perform an opening routine. They turn on all the equipment: ovens, fryers, flat-tops, and hoods. They deliver health code supplies to every section: sanitizer buckets, latex gloves, fancy caps, and probes. They re-up the stations with all the basics: pepper mills and saltshakers, as well as ninth pans for mise en place and squeeze bottles for fats and acids. In your walkthrough, you double-check this work. You also double-check the work of the cooks from the night before, their scrupulousness with the closing procedures. You make sure that any mise en place left over in their low-boys from last night has been consolidated, properly labeled, and neatly organized. You make sure that their ovens and fridges have been thoroughly cleaned. You make sure that the prep lists they've written for themselves are clear and comprehensive. Then you check the equipment. You make sure that all the fridges are holding a temperature below 40°F, to prevent bacterial development. You make sure that all the pilot lights are lit and that the burners are running clear. You make sure that all the hand sinks are stocked with soap and C-folds, that they're streaming both hot and cold water, and that their drain screens are free of debris. Finally, you make sure that all the hinges, handles, knobs, gaskets, and spouts are gunk-free, that everything, every corner, every tabletop, every surface, looks ship-shape, like new, next to godliness. These are the conditions we need in order to cook well.

After the line, it's time to hit the storage fridges — the walk-in boxes. The watchwords here are the same as on the line — cleanliness and order — but each walk-in also requires its own specific attention.

You start with the fish box. A briny waft

of sea air strikes you as you enter. This is good. If another aroma hits you — of chemicals, say, or rot — you know something is wrong, perhaps expensively so. Fish is the most delicate of all foodstuffs in the kitchen. It has the shortest shelf life, the highest price tag, and the weakest constitution. The flesh is easily damaged, and exposure to temperature fluctuations can denature its physical properties. It easily takes on an unattractive "fishy" smell. It becomes mealy. It develops slime. Not only do these transformations happen quickly, but they can also be of great detriment to the cooking process. The minutest degradation of quality impacts the ability of a given piece of fish to undergo the administration of heat. It loses its capacity to retain moisture; it fails to take a sear; it crumples, falls limp, goes floppy. This can harm the business significantly. There is an expectation among discerning diners that fish be cooked to perfection. In their minds, it is a chance for the chef to exhibit his skill, or lack thereof. People know that cooking beautiful fish at home presents a marked degree of difficulty. It breaks apart; it dries out; it's flavorless. It sticks, even to nonstick pans. When people go to a restaurant, they expect to see a better performance. The fact is, fish is always difficult, even for professionals. To be *chef poissonnier* in a good restaurant requires extensive experience and mastery of technique. It is one of the most honorable positions on the line, and for good reason. To complicate the exercise by allowing the protein to deteriorate through negligent storage can be ruinous.

So when you enter the fish box, you're checking on several things:

First is temperature. Whereas most foodstuffs keep well below 40°F, the fish box must remain between 34°F and 38°F.

Next is the manner of storage. All fish must be properly covered, protected from air, and shrouded with an abundance of ice. Whole fishes must be sitting upright in the ice — dorsal fins to the sky as if they were swimming — in order to preserve their anatomical constitution. Laying a whole fish on its side predisposes it to bruising, bone breaks, bloodline punctures, uneven air circulation, and a host of other unwanted conditions that compromise the integrity of the fish. Portioned fishes, on the other hand, must be wrapped tightly with food-service film, laid out flat and even in perforated trays (which keep liquids from pooling), and overspread with ice. Any deviations from these methods of storage must be rectified at once.

Next is the quality of the product. Everything must look fresh and smell fresh, or else it goes in the garbage.

Finally comes general hygiene. All surfaces — shelves, walls, ceilings, and floors — must be spotlessly clean. The fish box, above all places, must be immaculate.

The other boxes come under a similar level of scrutiny. The produce box should smell of fruits and vegetables, the dairy box should smell of milk and cheese, the beverage box should smell of beverages — typically keg beer, which can be nauseating in the morning — and the meat box should smell of blood. Like the lowboys on the line, all these boxes should be below 40°F. The standard pathogens — *Clostridium botulinum, Listeria monocytogenes, Trichinella spiralis, Escherichia coli,* salmonella, etcetera — have difficulty thriving under 40°F.

In the case of produce, everything should be properly kitted up in plastic containers. Fresh lettuce glows green in Lexans, gold bar squash shines in Cambros. Every container should be easily visible and clearly labeled with its contents, the packing date, and the initials of the handler. If the product has not been properly organized in a "first in, first out" fashion, you should be able to identify the issue immediately and correct it without difficulty.

In the dairy box, your focus is on expiration dates. A major error to look out for when the deliveries have been unpacked is the placement of new milk in front of old milk on the shelf. It's an easy corner that's often cut. The way to solve the problem is to figure out who's responsible for the error and bring him into the box to observe the situation. You might even read him the riot act. He'll likely snicker or apologize, blame somebody else, and fix it.

In the beverage cooler, you check the inventory. While it's usually the duty of the bar manager to maintain the beverage cooler, you keep your eye on certain pars, such as bar fruit and juices. Additionally, you check the bottled beer for evidence of tampering. Most missing beers in the restaurant are blamed on the kitchen staff — your staff. A bottle here or there is usually no cause for concern, but you check to ensure nothing's gotten out of hand.

You have one main objective in the meat box: to keep the chicken below and separate from everything else. Owing chiefly to production methods in most American bulk chicken facilities, the Department of Health considers the bird a terribly dangerous creature. It marinates in its own filth from the time it dies until the time you put it in the oven. It is a haven for bacteria. And its exudate — chicken juice — travels like quicksilver. No other protein can cross-contaminate its neighbors quite like chicken. When you enter the box, you make sure the chicken is never above and nowhere near anything else.

Likewise, you ensure that the eggs are safe. An intact egg is relatively innocuous. The expected bacterial distribution in industrially produced eggs is one contaminated unit per twenty thousand. Once that egg breaks, however, the potential for contamination spikes remarkably, as does the capacity for that contamination to spread, making the egg, too, a considerably dangerous entity. And so the Department of Health levies steep fines against restaurants for broken eggs. You take care in the meat box to check all the eggs.

When you are satisfied with the state of all the boxes, you go to task on checking the deliveries held therein. Overnight stewards and A.M. prep cooks are usually responsible for unpacking the deliveries, and they've been trained on how to put things away properly. But if something is amiss, the hammer will come down on you, so it is essential, again, to double-check their work.

For this you need the invoices, which are usually in Rogelio's custody. He will have decorated each invoice with check marks next to all the items that have arrived. You confirm with him that everything *seemed* to come in. He undoubtedly says yes, but you go through the invoices with a careful eye anyway. Often something will appear in one area of the invoice as delivered, but on spare sheets in the back it will be marked "unavailable" or "out of stock." This happens most frequently in dry storage and with exotic produce items. Even though you might order and receive such items all the time, they are often secretly unavailable, which is to say: special-order. Just because violet mustard and crosnes *seem* to be readily available doesn't mean that a given purveyor keeps them stocked in the regular catalog. It's not uncommon to get shorted on things like this from time to time, especially when they require importing.

You also always have to check the invoices against the order sheets that the closing sous chef prepared the night before, to ensure that nothing extra was delivered. This is another phenomenon that the A.M. prep cooks and stewards are typically unaware of, but a technique that some purveyors enjoy utilizing. Sales reps are often held to delivery minimums, which they might not tell you about in order to keep your transactions smooth and comfortable. On some occasions, though, when your order is shy of that minimum, they'll sneak something they know you use regularly onto the truck for you in order to prevent their bosses from taking it out on them. If this error has occurred, you call that particular purveyor on the phone, communicate your feelings about the matter aggressively, and insist that they retrieve the unneeded product and strike it from your invoice. If that hasn't occurred, however — if you've received everything that's been ordered and nothing else — you complete the invoices with a signature of approval and put them in a file with the rest of the week's paperwork.

Then, when the line is set and the fridges are clear and the deliveries have been meticulously checked, you do a final pass of the kitchen, making sure that all cardboard has been broken down, all trash has been bagged and taken out, all floors have been swept and mopped and are sparkling.

And like that, you're done with rounds.

It's ten-thirty now. Probably just enough time for one more cigarette before Chef arrives.

FINESSE JOBS

On your way out to the loading dock, you're met by your fellow sous, Stefan, who's on his way in. He's just been smoking himself — you can smell it on his fluffy parka. He decides to join you for another one. His breath smells of whiskey; his eyes are blood-shot. He was out last night. You sit on greasy milk crates and talk about it.

"Bro, shoeless drunk," he says, blowing a pair of smoke tusks out his nostrils. "Completely shitballs wasted."

It's morning still and neither of you wants to discuss service yet. Instead, you chat about what happened at the bars after work, share gossip about coworkers. The food service industry is incredibly incestuous, and licentious things are always happening between colleagues after service. Stefan regales you with the evening's inanities.

You stamp out the cigarettes and head in. While Stefan changes beside you in the confined office — his bristly skin stretching and puckering just inches from your face — you sit at the computer and check on the numbers for the night. It comes as no surprise that the cover count is at two hundred and rising. You knew when you woke up that it was going to be busy. It's Friday night. This is your reality.

"Yo, is this the Brinata?" he says, picking up the sample of cheese. "Nice, guy."

He cuts himself a wedge. You give him the breakdown.

Rogelio has been hard at work since 0600 and he's gotten us off to a good start. The herbs are snipped, the garlic is peeled, the baby vegetables have been turned. The stocks are up and the chicken bones have been roasted for the Château-Chalon. The demi-glace is reducing. The shrimps are peeled and deveined. Croquettes are being formed. Brianne, the P.M. prep cook, is due in at noon and she's scheduled to start immediately on the tomato confit. The prep lists that hang over the individual stations are side work for the cooks who are assigned to work there tonight. Items such as *pommes purees, soubise,* and other garnishes are the daily responsibilities of the *entremetiers* and will be completed closer to service, when they arrive in the afternoon.

The majority of the meat fabrication is in the hands of Julio, our swarthy *rôtisseur,* who should be in by 1300 to set up his station. Much of the heavy lifting has been delegated down the hierarchy by rote. The only tasks that fall to you and Stefan are the finesse jobs: butchering the fish, rolling out the pasta, generating the specials. It's up to the two of you who does what.

You start by sifting through the house to see what needs to be used up, burned out. There is a separate walk-in box in the back prep area devoted to prep work — the production box. Sauces, garnishes, dressings, cooked soups, cut vegetables, and so forth all reside here. Without regular attention, the production box has a tendency to become a garbage dump for leftover mise en place. As such, it is the perfect place to initiate the creative process, to seek inspiration for specials. There is a quart of salsa verde tucked behind containers of chive oil; a six-quart Cambro of beluga lentils hides in the back; a can of piquillo peppers has been opened, half used, and dumped into pints; a tray of boquerones, mummified in plastic wrap, has found its way to the top shelf. Ideas begin to take shape in your head. There is an unclaimed lobe of foie gras in the meat box; fresh herring in the fish box will turn if unused; Piave, Taleggio, and Scamorza collect dust in the dairy box; there are girolles and velvet foots; there are the Brinata, the PX, the pistachios . . . It excites you to imagine what Chef might come up with for tonight. But since he has the final say on what goes out to the dining room, no real work on the specials will get done until he arrives. And since you have to be doing something when Chef walks in, it behooves you to get started on the two major tasks: one of you will do the pasta, the other will do the fish.

Stefan asserts that he'd like to make the pasta. "Because," he says, "I'm better at it than you are. Your shit is mad doughy. Mine is elegant." His real motive is to hide out in the prep kitchen all day. Pasta, of course, is a time-consuming process, but it requires little physical effort. It's simple and relaxing. A hungover sous chef could immerse himself in the task all afternoon without having to reveal to Chef the state he's in. Which is just as well as far as you're concerned, because you consider fish butchery a specialty.

Stefan plucks a Pedialyte from the miniature refrigerator and sets off toward the back prep area. You pull a bib apron over your head and ready your knives.

■ ■ ■ ■

Proper butchery takes place behind the plastic-flap doorway of a chilled butcher's room. The room should be equipped with a deep sink, firm tables, and large, flat, self-healing cutting boards. Band saws, meat hooks, and other nifty gadgetry are helpful and often necessary in larger operations, but our restaurant doesn't generate the sort of business that necessitates massive amounts of protein fabrication, so we don't have them. In fact, we don't even have a separate room for butchery. Having seen such rooms before, however, you do your best to replicate the environment.

On a level stainless worktable, away from the ambient heat of the ranges on the line, you begin to set your workspace. You stretch a damp side-towel flat against the metal of the table, smoothing out any wrinkles, and place your cutting board on top of it to prevent the board from slipping. To the right are a stack of extra side-towels, latex gloves, fish tweezers, and a plastic container of water into which you will discard any pin bones. Above your board is a stack of empty stainless-steel half hotel pans of various depths, into which you will load the fabricated fish when you finish portioning it. Beside the pans is a gram-sensitive digital scale, which you will use to check your cuts for consistency and accuracy. To the left you've reserved a spot for the trays of fish that you will bring out from refrigeration successively as you are ready to work on them. Nearby are a roll of plastic wrap, a container of ice, and a slim-jim trash bin.

The knives you have brought out from your kit are your specialty fish knives: the Yo-Deba, the Petty, and the Sujihiki. Like any diligent chef, you'll take them to a stone before even thinking of cutting fish. But you sharpen your knives daily, so all they need is a few passes on eight-thousand grit to buff the edge to a shiny finish. The process is sensuous. They are obedient as you glide them across the smooth, wet surface of the stone. They're lined with a slim glister in no time — keen as razors. You fell a few scraps of paper to loosen any burr. The paper flutters to bits at the blades' touch. They are like katana. You are ready to cut the fish.

The first fish you retrieve from the box is the fluke, a flat whitefish native to the Atlantic waters just off the Long Island coast. Its flesh is a shady pearl color, moist and delicate. Its average weight is two or three pounds, but it can reach ten. It is sturdier than most fish its size, and it stands up to many cooking techniques. It is flaky and meaty at the same time. Its flavor welcomes bold combinations but stands as well on its own. It is versatile and delicious. Fluke is your favorite fish.

The spinal cord of the fluke runs directly down its middle. Whereas round fish are broken up bilaterally into a left and a right side, flatfish such as halibut and fluke can be seen as having four separate quadrants: top left, top right, bottom left, and bottom right. Unfortunately, this type of fish allows the careless butcher to carve out four fillets without betraying a lack of ability to the untrained eye. You know, however, that a true craftsman with careful knife work maintains the connection between the two sides of the top half and the two sides of the bottom half. You know to trace the tip of your blade carefully along the spine of the fish at the center, so as to preserve the membrane of skin between the cuts, allowing the fillets to retain their complete cellular integrity and yielding the amplest, supplest harvest of flesh. You try very hard every time you butcher fluke to achieve that. It's almost a competition you have with yourself. Which is why you'll cut fish before rolling pasta any day.

Your station is fully set, and the first fluke is on your cutting board. You take a deep breath and start in.

The first stroke of your knife glides hilt deep into the flesh of the fish. You can feel bone on your tip. You begin to trace the spine.

But a clattering at the back door interrupts your work.

"What's up, bitches!" booms a familiar voice from the entryway.

You glance up from the cutting board. It's the executive chef. Stefan materializes from the back prep area in a flash.

"What's up, Chef," you say, in unison.

"Good news," says Chef, tinkering on his BlackBerry. "We got a twelve-top at nine o'clock, followed by the *Times* at nine-thirty. We're at two fifty and climbing."

Your knife wavers in your hand. You nick the flesh of the fish inadvertently — a letdown. Chef's lips peel back like the Cheshire cat's.

"You boys ready to get your shit pushed in?"

THE TEAM

A kitchen's identity is shaped mainly by two things: cuisine and technique — what you cook and how you cook it. They are the obvious differences from one place to the next — Japanese or Italian, say, four-star or greasy spoon. But there are other, less obvious differences as well. The layout, for example, is always unique. The storage spaces, the walk-in boxes, the prep area, the line — they're positioned differently everywhere you go. Some kitchens have several floors and several rooms devoted to different tasks (pastry shops, sous vide labs, banquet lines, butcheries); other kitchens cram all the tasks into one space. The size and shape of things vary as well. Some spaces are big enough to hold eighty cooks at once; in other places you might cook through an entire night of service without leaving a four-by-four-foot space. In the big places, you use double-stacked combis —

computerized super ovens — to make huge batches of things; in the small places you might do everything to order on one six-burner range. Some restaurants are all about volume, turn-and-burn operations where all that matters is the Z report — the financial breakdown at the end of the day; other restaurants focus on the food and the ambiance, exchanging high cover counts for the quality of the experience. Some places can do both simultaneously; such places tend to do well.

Our restaurant is on the finer end of the spectrum. It's a "Modern American" eatery, tucked into the first floor of an old apartment building on a quiet street in the West Village. We have ninety seats in the dining room and about a dozen more at the bar. We have a small à la carte menu and we do half a dozen plats du jour. Our check average is around $75.00 per person (appetizer, entrée, dessert), plus drinks. We do a turn and a half most weeknights — about a hundred fifty covers, on average — and double that on Friday and Saturday. Monday through Friday we're dinner only, but we open up for brunch on the weekends.

We don't quite have the budget to be the *finest* of the fine, but we do what we can to approximate it. Of the three owners, one is a former chef, so a large chunk of the start-up capital went to outfitting our roughly two-thousand-square-foot kitchen with everything we need. All our equipment is kept in peak working condition, bought new, and well maintained. We don't fight with finicky pilot lights, our pipes don't clog, and our refrigerators' compressors don't ice over. When a lightbulb goes out, we change it, and if one of the tiles on the wall gets chipped, we have it fixed. We keep the inside of our ovens as clean as the day we got them, and we sweep and mop the floor constantly. Suffice it to say we have our heads on straight.

It's not uncommon in kitchens like this to find guideposts hanging here and there — "Make It Nice," for example, or "fi·nesse (fə-'nès) *noun:* Refinement and delicacy of performance, execution, or artisanship," or some inspirational verse from this or that esteemed culinarian — which remind hard-working cooks to stay focused on what they came here to do. On the tiled wall above the entrance to our kitchen hangs a placard done up in bold print that reads:

Under this banner marches a group of cooks who resemble the cliché: defiant types with tattoos and chin stubble, carved faces and bags under the eyes; muscle-backed bruisers with dancers' feet and calloused hands, arms burned hairless and shiny fingernails bitten to the quick. They are what anyone who's watched a cooking program or read a chef memoir would expect of a kitchen staff. But behind the common façade lies an array of unique personalities.

Bryan, our executive chef, is a thirty-eight-year-old Brooklyn native with chin-length hair and a taste for Glen Garioch. He's at least half a foot taller than most of the people you know — a lofty six foot five — and his arms and legs are tight with muscles from more than twenty years of service. But two decades of rich food have left his egg-shaped torso appropriately soft to the touch.

A precocious youngster, he dropped out of school at sixteen and moved to Paris. He studied at Le Cordon Bleu and did a four-year tour of apprenticeships at three-star restaurants in France, England, and Italy. That was the way young cooks used to do it: go to Europe, work eighteen hours a day, come back a better person. His was the generation that learned to cook by getting yelled at and pushed around by bulldog chefs in exchange for room and board and a glass or two of wine.

When he got back to America, he didn't waste any time. Within weeks he fixed himself a position on the line at an au courant French house specializing in fish cookery. They had three stars in the Michelin Guide and four in the *Times*. By twenty-three, he was *chef de cuisine* there, second in command, leaving a trail of dejected strivers in his wake. Fluency in the language, European training, and a sadistic approach to competition helped him more than just a bit. A native misanthropy made it easy for him to stop caring about the throats he had to cut on the way to the top. Since then, he's never looked back, helming several of his own places ranging from dives in Williamsburg to posh spots uptown. He's traveled the country consulting on everything from restaurant openings to commercial mustard production.

With such a pedigree, it's easy to wonder why he's here now, at this midsize restaurant in the West Village that's lucky to clear a couple million a year, when he could be making well into six figures in an easygoing position in corporate consulting or as a television personality. Here he works seventy-five-hour weeks, brings in about eighty grand, and deals every day with the incessant budgetary constraints, the half-baked floor staff, and the nettlesome hipster critics common to any midrange star-rated restaurant. For your average forward-looking cooks and chefs, these are simply the conditions of development, burrs under the saddle to be shed with growth in the industry. We fantasize about what great space and equipment and freedom we'll have in our future fine-dining restaurants. We grin and bear the daily struggle with the conviction that there is something better a few years down the road. But Bryan, whose foot-long résumé shames all of ours, grapples with the difficulties still. And he seems to do so by choice.

You could say that he does so because a place of this size allows him to realize a vision — a luxury that the big paycheck of a larger operation might not afford him. In a corporate restaurant, the food he'd make wouldn't be his, it'd be the company's. To even get a dish on the menu at such a place requires an elaborate process of hoop jumping. Tastings with the director of food and beverage, with the corporate chef, with the national director of restaurants — it's bureaucracy at its messiest. By the time a new dish arrives on the menu, it's lost all traces of spontaneity and freshness. It's gone stale. So you could say that Bryan is here because he has a special vision of how food is supposed to be made and he likes getting to do it that way every day.

You could also say that he does it because he is a chef of the kitchen, a chef who cooks, too. That is to say, he's here because he *wants* to be here, in the flames, in the heat, on the line. He is captivated by the act of cooking, by the warmth that comes off the stove, by the sweat that comes with a full day of work. He likes having his hands on everything, his fingers in all the pies. And he knows that here, unlike the corporate kitchen (where the majority of one's days are spent in the office analyzing invoices and managing food cost), here he actually gets to cook things.

Or perhaps you could say it's something else. He is getting old in chef years, after all; perhaps he's burning out. Perhaps it's his only option. This happens sometimes in restaurants: a decade goes by and business dwindles. Ten years in this industry is like two dozen in another. The food one makes might still be great (a chef's instincts stay with him always), but after so many years, customers inevitably grow tired of his fare. They want what's cutting-edge, not the dusty old names of decades past. And with each passing year, staying ahead of the curve becomes harder and harder. So the chef gives the restaurant up, jumps ship. But what awaits him? His cook's pittance is nothing to retire on; he has to keep working. All he knows is cooking, so he stays in the business. But since his name no longer attracts the avant-garde food enthusiasts, he does his cooking at a lower volume in smaller places — trattorias, bistros, ateliers — where he can engage the act of cooking and explore his curiosities without the same level of pressure intrinsic to high-budget establishments. He retires out of fine dining proper and into the small, privately owned house.

With Bryan, it's hard to say which of these conditions apply. He's still full of piss and vinegar over cooking; you can tell that he loves the process. And he certainly doesn't lack energy in the kitchen, or creative ebullience. But the gray hairs nested around his ponytail, his ruddy skin, the distant look in his eyes when he slaps you up and says "See you in the morning" — these tell a different story. Like most people in his position, he's difficult to read.

Whatever the case may be, he's here now and he is Chef. And when he's in the kitchen and the whites are on, it is embarrassing to think of addressing him any other way. There is no "Bryan" in the kitchen — no "Bry," no "man" nor "dude" nor "buddy" — only Chef. He is the lodestar, the person everyone looks up to. He commands respect and exudes authority. His coats are crisp and clean, his pants are pressed, his hair is tied back neatly. He has more experience than anyone else in the kitchen; he knows more about food than anyone else in the kitchen; he can cook better than anyone else in the kitchen. He is the best butcher; he is the best baker. He's the sheriff, the chief, the maestro. He choreographs. He directs. He makes the difficult look easy. His finesse is ubiquitous.

And then, what would any great leader be without his second in command? In a chef's case, this is his sous chef. The sous chef (from the French meaning "under chef") is the lieutenant, the executor of Chef's wishes. He is at Chef's side seventy hours a week or more, for good or for bad, a perpetual Mark Antony to Chef's Julius Caesar. Out of this devotion grows a lasting bond.

A chef always looks out for his sous chef; a sous is always "under" his chef's wing — guided, nurtured, cared for, long after the stoves are turned off and the aprons are hung up. While other cooks are apprenticed to the kitchen, the sous is apprenticed directly to Chef. He is not there to learn how to cook properly or how to organize a restaurant — he is expected to have these skills already. Instead, the sous works with Chef on developing leadership, moxie, brio — the subtler elements of the craft. He's not just learning how to be a cook, he's learning how to become a chef. And at this point in his career he is one rung away from that achievement.

The position can be difficult. It requires a peculiar disposition that is foreign to most. Not only does it entail a uniquely large amount of physical labor — twelve to fifteen hours per day, six or seven days per week — but also it engenders a certain kind of ambivalence. That limbo between cook and chef, where the taste of clout is tempered yet by the burden of compliance, is no easy place to dwell, especially for the veteran sous. The gratitude and pride intrinsic to the appointment are not without some tinge of bitterness; the excitement of power is not without a trace of fear. To wit, *you* want to be Chef. You want *your* name on the menu. You're tired of doing all the work and getting none of the recognition. Yet deep down you wonder if you're really ready to assume all the responsibility that comes with authority, to take all the blame that goes along with credit. It's a charge replete with dualities, and at the end of the day you're left straddling the fulcrum, made to decide for yourself whether the student in you has what it takes to become the master.

In our kitchen, as in many others like it, there are two sous chefs: you and Stefan. To those unfamiliar with it, a setup like this might seem dangerous. Having a pair of lieutenants could be fertile earth for competition — who outranks whom, for example, who is the real right-hand man. But you know there is no room for rivalry in this part of the kitchen. The two of you represent the upper echelon and you must work in concert with each other, and with Chef as well, to form a unified corps of governance. Your cohesion as a group is crucial to the fluid operation of the restaurant. Dissension among you will undoubtedly lead to ruin: recipes get garbled, techniques and attitudes begin to vary among the cooks, consistency diminishes, and ultimately the restaurant goes bust. So you do well as members of the sous chef team to reserve your competitive zeal for the outside world.

Fortunately, each of you serves a distinct function for Chef. Like knives in a tool kit, he's selected you individually based on certain character traits that satisfy specific needs of his. You each help complete the kitchen's picture with specialized contributions.

At the most basic level, you are the opener and Stefan is the closer. You come in earlier; Stefan stays later. What this means is that Chef trusts you to arrive on time in the morning and get everything set for dinner service. He expects you to handle the detail-oriented matters of purchasing and receiving, inventory and organization. He expects you to turn the kitchen's lights on. Because of you, he can wake up in the morning without worrying that some emergency requires his presence at the restaurant. He knows that you are here and so he can take his time getting in because, it's assumed, you have everything under control.

He also has you opening because he knows your penchant for creativity, your gastronomical curiosity. Being the opener affords you the opportunity to help with the specials. Since you take the morning inventory and do all the purchasing, you are the one most fully aware of what we have in-house, you know what needs to be used up and burned out. And so, typically, when Chef comes in, he sits you down in the office and ruminates with you about what to do for service. The two of you brainstorm, philosophize, think about what's possible in cooking.

The last, and likely most important, reason he has you opening is purely administrative. Since you have extra time during the day as the opener, and since your attention to detail has proved unflinching, he entrusts you with the payroll and the making of the schedule. Not only does this charge acquaint you with the logistical matters associated with operating a restaurant, but also it puts you in unique contact with the cooks. You are responsible for their schedules, so they come to you with requests and conflicts. You are also responsible for their paychecks, so they come to you with gripes. If they want overtime, they ask you; if they need an advance to cover rent, they ask you. You hold the key to their livelihood, and so you act as a sounding board for their financial woes.

Stefan's position is different. He is the enforcer, the wiry disciplinarian. He has hewn closely to the gold standard of the modern high-order professional kitchen: go hard or go home. He has gone hard since the outset.

By the time he was sixteen, Stefan, a zealous Virginian, had already beaten a path up Hyde Park way. There was no career he was willing to entertain other than cooking and, in his mind, there was no better place to begin pursuing that career than the Culinary Institute of America. When externship season came rolling around, he shot straight for the top, and he hasn't looked back. He cut his teeth at all the city's best restaurants and continues to maintain a dogged resistance to dipping below three stars. He's always checking the listings to see who is opening what and where; he's always looking for the next hot spot, the next great opportunity. And he'll take it, too, if it seems like a step forward in his career. He is a soldier of fortune, a survivor, and every success he's enjoyed thus far he's achieved by dint of pure tenacity.

His attraction to fine dining makes him the perfect disciplinarian. The only environment he knows is one of utmost intensity. He holds himself and those around him to the highest standard of performance imaginable, and Chef trusts him to preserve that standard at every turn. Although he may look a bit loose at the seams — perpetually scruffy, routinely hungover — he is incapable of doing things inelegantly on the line. He's a prodigy on the stove, an ace on the pass. And he simply *does not know how* to conceal his disdain for poor technique. When a cook mishandles a situation, Stefan is usually the first to point it out, loudly and churlishly. He is cutthroat in this respect, and most of the cooks have grown to fear encounters with him.

Right beneath the sous chefs are the lead cooks, the big guns. They tend not to respond to Stefan's antagonism. These are the people who cook the meat to the right temperature and handle the fish properly — the *rôtisseurs* and *poissonniers.* They are the cream of the cooks and they know it, one short step away from management. As such, their jobs require the most skill and trust, and more often than not, the most experience. They are typically older, more graceful, more powerful cooks with booming voices and a due sense of self-worth.

Julio, our *rôtisseur,* is a forty-year-old Dominican who speaks perfect English and takes insolence from nobody. You never have to worry about him. He is the first to the pass on every pick. His temperatures are always perfect. He eighty-sixes nothing. He gets the job done. And the poise and pride with which he comports himself, combined with his preternatural skills in meat cookery, amount to the perfect recipe for upward mobility, should he ever decide to take the next step in his career.

But Julio is one of those cooks who are content to remain on the line rather than move up the chain. Professional cooking is just something he has always done for work. It is a trade to him, an occupation more than a vision quest. His priorities are elsewhere. He is married, he has children, he owns a home. It seems that his life is full in the outside world, that he's happy with it the way it is. And the gold wedding ring he wears while he works serves as a perpetual reminder of that.

Raffy, our *poissonnier,* is of a similar mold. Like Julio, he is phenomenal at what he does. Hailing from Basque country, he, like Chef, has European training, mostly French and Spanish. He is accustomed to long hours and high expectations. His ability with fish is surpassed perhaps only by Chef's, and his sweeping knowledge of archaic technique (how to flute a mushroom, for example) is enough to incite jealousy.

Unlike Julio, though, Raffy seems fundamentally attracted to professional ascension. He is a sprightly twenty-something anxious to move up the ranks. He really wants to be a chef. And, based on ability alone, he should be. He should have nabbed at least a sous chef position by now. As it stands, however, he remains cloistered on fish roast. It's his attitude that's the problem. He's been known to leave his station a mess at the end of the night; he shows up late from time to time; he tends to petulance when it gets busy; he gravitates toward alcohol after service perhaps a bit too frequently. Simply put, he is immature. So, while he might *want* to be a chef some day, he's going to need to button a few things up if he ever hopes to actually get there.

Below the lead cooks are a group that do tend to respond to Stefan's derisive approach. They are the vegetable cooks — the *entremetiers.* They are responsible for the "middle work," which can be very intense. Most of the components on a given plate are prepared by the entremets. For every steak Julio broils or every fish Raffy sears, his respective entremet prepares anywhere from two to twelve garnishes — vegetables, starches, sauces, salads, etcetera. Leaving off the actual proteins, anything in a dish that needs to be sautéed, wilted, steamed, stirred, toasted, folded, roasted, tossed, shaved, pressed, grated, dressed, salted, seasoned, or otherwise treated before it reaches Chef's hands is the duty of the *entremetier.*

This can be a special challenge in a restaurant where everything is prepared to order — *à la minute.* Your average entremet is accustomed to managing fifteen or twenty separate pans of food at once. As a result, usually only the most motivated cooks can work the *entremetier* station. They are typically young, exuberant cooks with a few years of experience, in the early stages of their development.

Warren and Vinny do this work for us. While their titles are basically the same, they as people could not be more dissimilar.

Warren, an early-thirties curly blond, is our entremet on fish side. He is one of these late bloomers who come to cooking by vocation after an unsuccessful attempt at another career. He studied entomology at Cornell and worked for years in the profession before first taking to the stove. But since his arrival here about six months ago, he's shown an incredible amount of development. He truly wants to be here, almost

71

needs to be here, and he tries very hard to be as good a cook as he can be. His manner is decorous, his station is spotless, he strives to impress, he is diametrically opposed to sloth, and he *hates* failure. The cooks call him Juan. Chef Juan, Don Juan, Juanita, Juan Gabriel, etcetera. It started with a general unfamiliarity with the name Warren — Kiko just thought the guy's name was Juan. But now, though the misunderstanding has long been ironed out, everyone continues to call him that, even the white guys. They're just razzing him, of course, but Warren's really bugged by it.

Unlike Warren, Vinny or VinDog, our meat entremet, could not care less what people think of him. A brick shithouse with beefy arms and a bad attitude, VinDog is animated always by some urgent, unquenched irreverence. His neck is tattooed, his face is pierced, and something resembling a Mohawk has been sawn into his head. At first glance, he's not what you'd expect to find lurking in the wings of a star-rated restaurant.

Nor does he appear to be here because he needs to be. He doesn't need a restaurant to line his pockets or fill his spirit — he's happy to get his share by hook or crook. But apparently he prefers cooking to, say, working construction or collecting trash. So about a year ago, when Chef offered to extricate him from a bar-backing gig in Alphabet City, VinDog saw fit to seize the opportunity. Had things gone differently, you'd probably find him slapping up Sheetrock in Chinatown or circling the drain somewhere in Bushwick. It's questionable, actually, if his real name is even Vinny.

But VinDog exemplifies a fairly common contradiction. Beneath the ragamuffin façade is an intelligent, curious, resourceful person, almost custom-made for the kitchen. He takes hard work like water off a duck's back and he never stops asking questions until he gets the answers he needs. While his street clothes may be dirty, his work is always clean; while his appearance may be suspect, his cook's chops are nonpareil. That he owes his skill-set entirely to Chef's mentoring is undoubted, but that he is able to survive in this environment speaks to his own adaptability and to that of the kitchen as well.

Below Warren and VinDog is Catalina, our garde manger. Garde mangers are the salad cooks, the appetizer specialists. They are usually entry-level line cooks, working out of a satellite station alongside pastry on the cold side. They prepare mostly small cold items such as hors d'oeuvres, *amuse-bouches,* and salads, with occasional responsibility for desserts. They have less seniority than the cooks on the hot side, but they almost always outrank the guys back in prep. They *do* work the line, as it were, which is always a source of pride and some variety of authority in the kitchen hierarchy.

Five-two, buck-eighty, gold-toothed, and bangle-wristed, Catalina assumes all the authority she can muster. She epitomizes the hard-nosed constitution for which Mexican women are famous. She has come to be a sort of matriarch in our operation and, as is to be expected, she tackles her motherly duties vigorously. After her day off, she'll return to work with a stack of tortillas, a wheel of *queso fresco,* and a bushel of tomatillos and prepare *flautas con salsa verde* for the entire kitchen team. When someone burns or cuts himself, she is the first to arrive on the scene with ground pepper and tomato, to stop the bleeding, disinfect, and numb the pain. And on the unlikely occasion that a rodent should venture into the kitchen, she'll make quick work of taking it down — often grabbing it with her bare hands, muffling it up in a to-go bag, dispatching it with a whack or two on the ground, and pitching it into the dumpster out back of the loading dock.

Catalina is *esposa* to the A.M. prep cook, Rogelio; *tía* to the P.M. prep cook, Brianne; and *madre* to our favorite dishwasher, Kiko. They make a nice little family, the four of them, and they contribute a significant amount to our operation's skeletal system.

Rogelio, or Don Rojas, as we often refer to him, is indispensable. In addition to his duties receiving and unpacking deliveries, he's also responsible for the bulk of our production work. He takes care of the daily basics such as sliced garlic, peeled vegetables, and snipped herbs, which need to be ready by the time the cooks arrive. But his main area of focus is the large-format projects. We have him doing all our pickling and preserving, making all our stocks and bouillons, and, probably most important, maintaining many of our sous vide systems. He is responsible for most of the ROP and HACCP logging, for monitoring the pars on our compression and infusion projects, and for executing all our multiday braises. Without him, our sous vide output would be a fraction of what it is. Suffice it to say, we get to cook the way we do in large part because of the work that Rogelio does.

Brianne is equally vital. She arrives in the afternoon and carries us through to the bitter end. Her strength is batch work — the foodstuffs that get made every couple of days: aiolis, sofritos, vinaigrettes, etcetera — and she devotes most of her time to working on projects of this sort. She's possessed by a certain spirit of inquiry, so working with recipes and learning to perfect them is a main goal of hers. She is also ambitious to ascend the ranks, and it shows in her performance. Tireless, punctual (if not early), determined, eager, curious, never failing to lend a hand — these are only a few of the ways that Brie could be described. And it comes in handy, this work ethic of hers, especially on busy nights when the linesmen need to re-up on mise en place throughout service. Brie is the queen of ancillary prep work. She is always there to fill the gaps.

And then there is Kiko — our *chef plongeur.* The word "exhaustion" doesn't appear to be part of this man's lexicon. This is not uncommon among dishwashers — a steadfast devotion to hard, mindless labor, an appetite for constant activity. Kiko works basically around the clock washing dishes, putting in doubles most of the week. On top of that, he never turns down overtime. As a result, his paychecks are huge, which is probably why he is generally pleasant with everybody (except Raffy, whose insouciance toward the dish team seems to boil Kiko's blood). He's also the acting ambassador for the rest of the dish crew, which consists of an overnight steward, a weekend pot washer, and a pair of P.M. dish men, all of whom are seldom seen and even less frequently heard from.

Outside this core group of cooks and dishwashers, a few others join our team intermittently. We have the part-time pastry faction, consisting of a consulting pastry chef and baker, who come in extremely early on Mondays and Thursdays to set up the batters, doughs, and sauces for our dessert program; we have the *stagiaire* set, a regular rotation of cooking school externs who come in for a day or two at a time to study our technique; and we have the back waiters, a trio of low-ranking floor staffers led by Hussein, our Bengali *chef de rang*.

Back waiters are the unhailed linchpins of the dining experience. They are the people who run the food to the dining room and the people who bring back the empty plates. They are the ones who set the tables and the ones who clear them as well. They deliver glassware, light candles, refresh waters, and fetch sides of ketchup. And when a group of guests has left a table, they move quickly and efficiently to ready it for the next set. Simply put, they perform all the unobserved graces that diners have come to expect from restaurants. And whereas servers and bartenders and managers and maître d's represent the face of the restaurant — taking orders, fielding questions, explaining things to guests — the back waiters do their jobs in relative anonymity.

But the most important role the back waiters play is informant to the kitchen. They are our eyes and ears out front. They tell us which tables are ready for their next courses and which ones we should slow down on. They let us know what sections and servers are slammed and whom we can expect big tickets from soon. They notify us when important guests arrive and they remind us where they are sitting. They have the presence of mind to alert us when the dining room is filling up so we can be ready, and the kindness of heart to inform us when it is emptying out so we can begin breaking down. And, unlike most other FOH staff, who can sometimes get caught up coddling customers, back waiters always have time throughout service (and usually make it a point) to update us on how people seem to be enjoying their meals. Which is why, even though they are technically a constituent of the waitstaff, we often regard the back waiters as members of the kitchen team — an affiliation they readily accept. They are back here with us most of the night, working out of the limelight, so their allegiance lies with us.

With all these individuals scampering around during service, much can go wrong very quickly. It's a plate-spinning act, which could topple over in pieces at any moment. A chef's goal during any given meal period is to prevent this from happening — to sustain a fusion of all the moving parts, to keep the team together, to keep the bus driving straight. There will always be the clatter of pots and pans, the din of voices — professional cooking is a loud racket — but when service is performed fluidly, artfully, all the noise can be mistaken for silence. There's a certain harmony to the sound, and it's almost as though you don't even hear it.

Plats Du Jour

Of all the conditions that can disrupt a kitchen's harmony, anger is probably the most dangerous. There are many different types of anger in the kitchen, and each one manifests itself in a different way. Mistakes during service, for example, will always arouse immediate attack. If you break a plate, you will be called an idiot; if you drag on a pickup, you will be called a *tortuga;* if you overcook a piece of meat, you will be called a shoemaker. An especially charged service might aggravate the situation. When the dining room is full, say, or when a food critic is in the house, the stakes are high, and everyone tries very hard to make service perfect. At such moments, an error on your part might create an unnecessary emergency for someone else, and tempers may flare to even violent dimensions. Chef might throw a plate at you or trash your mise en place. He might drag you from the line by the scruff of your neck and throw you outside on the street. A line cook might shove past you in a huff, perhaps grazing your arm with a sizzle platter. A dishwasher might threaten to kill you. When the heat is on, everyone is at each other's throat.

But anger that arises during service is short-lived. It is the result of frenzy, and it's often forgotten before the last guest is served. Anger that arises before service, however, is a different beast. It is the slow burn, a wicked seed that sprouts like pea tendrils and strangles you until the end of the night.

When *you* are made angry before service — during your morning walk-through, say, or your afternoon prep — it is as though a small fire has been started somewhere in you that swells by the minute. A sense of increasing urgency accompanies each new task you take on, and before long you find yourself erupting vulgarly at the most insignificant things. You bump your head in the walk-in box and curse out the vegetables; your peeler slips and you rocket a handful of turnips into the trash. It's very easy, when you're busy and irritable, to begin believing that the whole world is against you. But it is critical at these moments to rein in your aggression, or else there might be serious consequences. Blue flames and steel blades don't forgive. If you allow your anger to distract you, you could burn or cut yourself. And, among serious cooks and chefs, burns and cuts are terribly unfashionable. The only thing worse than a burn or a cut is the need for medical attention. Abandoning your fellow linesmen because you lost focus and flayed a finger is an unforgivable offense.

To make someone *else* angry before service, though — especially if it's our capricious chef — can be pandemonic. Not only do you risk impairing the rapport of the cooks, but also you chance bringing out the despot in Chef, which invites a less obvious kind of stress into your day. It's not rage, but a dull, throbbing trepidation that takes hold, like a stiff neck that makes you fear turning your head the wrong way. You become preternaturally aware of Chef's location in relation to your own, expecting him to pop out at every turn and find you doing something improperly. You consider the possibility that all your technique is rubbish and that everyone knows it. Thinking about it makes it worse. A prep list becomes a minefield of possible mistakes, and the more concern you give each task, the longer each one takes, and the closer you get to service, and the less time you have, and the more stress you confront, and the more poorly you perform your work. It's an infinite regression.

And now Chef is heated. He went from jolly to crabby instantaneously when he found the samples you tasted torn open, chewed up, and scattered about the desk. The fact that they were opened doesn't matter to him, but the fact that they were left out has dialed him up. Sure, he's not the angriest you've ever seen him, but he certainly isn't happy. His mood has definitely shifted. You felt the elephant enter the room.

But isn't he overreacting a bit? The samples were free, after all, and failing to store them properly has no impact on the business, or even on an evening's service, for that matter. Nevertheless, in the mind of the chef, it is a failure. It is a betrayal of a certain trust and a disappointment of certain expectations. You should know better, and the fact that you don't reflects poorly on your character, and poorly on Chef even, because he thought you were better than that. And planting that seed now will influence his reaction to the little things later on. But it's a wheel of cheese and a sack of pistachios we're talking about here.

And it wasn't even you who left them out. Still, it should have been you who put them away.

This is where your mind wanders as you butcher the fish. Your hands are on autopilot — they slice and weigh and wrap and chill, portion after portion. But your brain is elsewhere, preoccupied with gauging Chef's level of anger. You want to know what to expect for the night, and in order to calculate that, you must first diagnose Chef's mood. The whole operation hinges on your relationship with him.

He hasn't said much. He hasn't asked you what needs burning out. He hasn't sat you down to bounce around ideas for specials. He certainly hasn't made conversation. He's distant, focused, in his own head, thinking about who knows what. And it seems he's been this way for hours. But the repetitive, meditative nature of butchery always modifies your concept of time. He hasn't even been here an hour yet. It's not even 1300 and he's already coming to you with the specials.

"All right, *papi chulo,*" he says, handing you a printout. "Let's get this party started. I got the terrine A to Z. You get started on the monkey and we'll see where we're at after that. You know how I like it. But don't fuck around. Check with me first before you start anything you haven't seen before. Make it nice not twice, right, baby?"

He claps you on the shoulder and walks away. His tone is heartening. You feel welcomed back into the fold. You smile and have a look at the plats du jour:

FRIDAY, DECEMBER 7
TERRINE OF BOUDIN BLANC AND
SQUAB CONFIT
rocket, filbert, quince, verjus

•

CHARRED HERRING
*mustard potato, pickled ramp,
boquerones fondue*

•

VEAL TONGUE AGNOLOTTI
*winter mushroom,
preserved lemon butter*

> ### MONKFISH ROULADE
> *foie gras, beluga lentil,*
> *endive, carrot, caraway*
>
> •
>
> ### BLACK HERITAGE PORK LOIN SOUS VIDE
> *guanciale, chestnut, turnip, sapori forte*

It is more than just a list of specials he's given you; it's punishment for your negligence with the samples. Your prep list has expanded logarithmically. With only four hours before service starts, pulling this whole menu together is nearly impossible, and he knows it. He is putting your mettle to the test. More important, he is seeing how well you can delegate responsibility.

If he is on the terrine, as he says he is, that leaves you with four dishes to gather. You'll get started on the monkfish, as he told you to, but not before resolving a couple of other issues first.

Stefan is in back on the pasta machine, so it makes sense to transfer the entire agnolotti dish to him directly. It's simple enough and he can do it all himself, hungover or not. He needs to make another batch of dough right now. After he's done rolling out the pasta for the regular menu, and by the time he's finished making the veal tongue farce, the new dough will have rested long enough, and he can sheet up the agnolotti. In the meantime, Rogelio can clean the mushrooms and brunoise the preserved lemon for him. He can handle the rest from there. If he has any questions, he can take them up with Chef.

"*Claro,* baby," Stefan says when you show him the menu. "I got that shit."

Now for the herring. You saw them in the fish box, but you can't remember if they are clean or not. It's safe to assume the worst, but safer still to not even worry about that now. Brianne can clean them later on, if necessary. More important to that dish are the potatoes. You know that when Chef says "mustard potatoes" he means essentially his version of a German potato salad: boiled potatoes tossed with whole grain mustard, truffles, and chives. In order for the potatoes to chill amply, they need to go up now. A quick glance at the menu indicates that they are probably the most urgent thing, so you grab a large rondeau and begin filling it with cold water. As the rondeau fills, you figure out the rest of the dish: the pickled ramps are already in the box left over from spring, so that's a no-brainer. You can imagine Chef will either fold them into the potato salad, or dot them around the plate, or whatever. If he wants to do something more extravagant with them, like puree them into a fluid gel, he can exercise the foresight to tell you. Otherwise, you'll run with the idea that the ramps are already done. As far as the sauce is concerned, you remember Chef telling you one time about his boquerones sauce, which is basically a beurre blanc with white anchovies, finnan haddie, and a touch of xanthan gum buzzed into it, which can be handled later, too. The rondeau is full now. You salt the water until it tastes like the sea, and then you load it up with potatoes and put it on the stove. You use fingerlings, of course, given that the only other potatoes in house are king-size Yukons and Idaho 90s. You approximate that you have enough sardines for twenty orders so you shoot for somewhere in the neighborhood of seven pounds of potatoes. You drop them in the water and throw the rig up on the stove.

Pork. The problem with this dish is Chef's sapori forte sauce. Rogelio has already started bringing down the demi-glace, so you're out of the woods there, but the rest of the mise en place is a little tricky — there are many components. You need to dig through the storeroom and find mustard oil, cornichons, and golden raisins, which you may or may not have. If you don't — which is a distinct possibility — it is your fault for not maintaining those pars and you will have to sneak to the store to buy some without telling Chef, which will be difficult because he'll see you leave. Beyond that you'll need to make a tarragon butter (for which you should get a couple of pounds of butter softening now) and slice the chestnuts ("the brain way," as Chef says — thin vertical slices that look like cross-sections of a brain). You'll also need a brunoise of carrot. But it has to be nice because the carrots, cornichons (which need to be sliced into rounds as well), and raisins are supposed to be decorative, so you can't have Rogelio or Brianne do it, because they'd mess it up. If one of the line cooks has a shorter list, you can make him do it. If not, it's going to fall on you or Stefan, which probably means it's going to fall on you. What the prep cooks can do, though, is prep the turnips. Regardless of what Chef plans to do with the turnips, you know no matter what that these steps will have to be taken. Whether they're warmed in soubise or seared in duck fat, they'll need to be peeled, turned, and blanched first, and you know he's not going to puree them because puree-ing baby turnips would be like cooking twenty quails for Thanksgiving instead of just making a turkey.

The protein, the actual pork itself, can be cleaned by Julio, whom you're pretty sure you just saw walk in. It just needs to be denuded, which is to say, boned, chined, and trimmed of its fat cap, so it shouldn't take him long. He's also plenty used to sous vide, so he can take care of vacuum-sealing the meat, and you can trust him to get it into the circulator on time so that it's fully thermalized by the time service starts. The only question mark is what Chef plans on doing with the guanciale. Perhaps he will dice it up and cook it with the turnips, but then the bits might get lost in the sapori forte. Perhaps he will make chips with it the way he makes salami chips, but then with the amount of fat that would melt away, you wouldn't get much yield, and so it would be cost-ineffective. Perhaps the best guess is that he plans to roll it into the bag with the pork loin before it gets vacked, to scent the loin with that distinctive aroma unique to guanciale. Either way, that's something you can ask him the next time you see him, but there's probably no reason to hunt him down right now.

Assuming again that Chef's got the terrine under control, all you're left with is the monkfish. Fortunately, you've made this dish with Chef before, so you know exactly what he is looking for; unfortunately, it's the most complicated dish.

The wording for dishes on the menu is slightly deceptive by intention. A good chef always strives to imbue the dining experience with an element of surprise. Provocative verbiage is one of the easiest ways to do this. While some eaters might go in for lavish description on a menu, the sagacious chef recognizes the power of concealment. It's a more tasteful approach, which excites a spark of curiosity in the adventurous diner when done right. This way, the arrival of the food presents a revelation to the diner, and the experience of finally decrypting the menu through actual ingestion allows for a welcome degree of what we'll call audience participation.

But you're an insider and these tricks don't fool you. You know that the "roulade" consists of not just the monkfish, as the title of the dish would have one believe, but also the foie gras and caraway mentioned with the garnish. It basically works like uramaki sushi (and requires about as much finesse to produce), where the flesh of the monkfish takes the place of the rice and the foie gras takes the place of the filling. You simply cut the monkfish into sheets, fit it with strips of foie gras, swab the concoction with a slurry of meat glue, and roll it up. The result is a shaft of protein that gets speckled with ground caraway, wrapped tightly in plastic, and placed under refrigeration to set.

Meat glue — known as transglutaminase in more sophisticated kitchens, or Activa in the purveyors' catalogs — is an enzyme that, when applied to two different cuts of meat, activates a covalent bond between the proteins, joining them together, in theory forever. The most notable feature of this transaction is its thermo-irreversibility — the fact that the bond formed is capable of withstanding the application of heat — which means that your meat-glued product will not break apart when you cook it, which makes the technique perfect for the monkfish roulade. The only rub is, the meat glue needs ample time to set up — at least four hours, generally — so you know that if you want to be ready for service, you'll need to get those roulades wrapped up on the double. This is especially problematic be-cause monkfish and foie gras take probably the most time to clean of anything in the kitchen. You take a breath and go to work.

Monkfish is the ugliest fish in the sea. Its skin is like mucus. It comes to you from the fishmonger with no head, no scales, and no pin bones, which is good, but you have to battle through two layers of slimy dermis before you get to the usable flesh. Because of its slippery texture, the skin is incredibly difficult to remove without damaging the meat, so you must take your time, and your knives must be razor-sharp. You must also keep several towels handy, because gobs of sticky skin will cling to everything near you.

When you do finally reach the flesh, removing it from the bone is effortless. A wide spine splits the fish in two lengthwise, and a drag of the knife down the vertebrae slices the meat off with ease. The resulting fillets are the size and shape of a small forearm.

Monk fillets are not flaky like regular fish, but meaty like lobster. Owing to the density of the flesh, careful knife work allows you to create your roulade sheets with a few simple glides of your Sujihiki. You press the fillet flat against the cutting board with your free hand and make a half-inch-deep incision, parallel to the tabletop, along its full length. Spread the incision, readjust the angle of the fillet against the board, and repeat the process. If done properly, the fillet should unroll like a scroll with a few quick passes. Your focus should be on the flatness and evenness of the sheet so as to facilitate the rolling process. The meat glue will rectify any errant cuts.

You cover the sheeted monkfish in plastic and place it under refrigeration to prevent bacterial development. At the same time, you remove the foie gras from refrigeration so it can temper. Meanwhile, the potatoes have finished as you were cutting the monkfish, so you shift your focus momentarily and get them out of the water and into the blast chiller so that they don't overcook. By the time you've finished tending to the potatoes, changing out your cutting board, and sanitizing your station, the foie will be the perfect consistency.

Cleaning foie gras is like performing an autopsy. A reticulum of unsavory blood vessels weaves among the edible material. It is important to remove all of them if you want to isolate the pure flavor and texture. To do so, you make a small slit at the nexus of the liver's hemispheres and carefully peel apart the lobes using your thumb and the spine of a Petty knife. The goal is to unwrap the liver like a delicate gift, so that the blood vessels remain intact. Many of the veins still have blood in them, which could stain the tan meat an unattractive pink, so it's important not to puncture them with the edge of your blade. It's also important that the organ retain the greatest level of structural integrity possible, for the sake of its freshness, cookability, and texture. To mash it to smithereens would be brutish and wasteful; it would defeat the purpose. It should look like a beautiful brown orchid when you are done. When you're satisfied that it is sufficiently clean, you roll it back up and place it in the fridge with the monkfish.

Suddenly you realize it is almost 1400. This task has taken you far too long. A show plate of each special is due up at 1630 so it can be explained to and tasted by the waitstaff during the premeal meeting. The time has come to begin delegating large chunks of work.

The first order of business is to account for all the proteins. Most important, of course, is to show Rogelio — who has hopefully finished turning the turnips, cleaning the mushrooms, and dicing the preserved lemon — how to roll the roulades. When you ask him to do it, he will probably make a stink about it, but if you can get him on your side, he'll stick around.

"I go home three o'clock," he says.

"I give you overtime, baby."

"Okay, Chef," he says. "I stay."

The pork is literally in Julio's hands. He's taken on the duty with a typical austerity and seems to be plugging through it at a good clip. He's cut the meat to size and has begun labeling the boilable sous vide bags with the appropriate HACCP information. It also appears that he has resolved the guanciale situation with Chef — it is going in the bag, too, as you suspected. He's also got a circulator bringing a water bath up to temperature. All he has to do now is seal the bags up in the Cryovac and take the little piggies for a swim.

You yourself have checked the herring and confirmed that they need to be cleaned, but you resign yourself to the fact that you'll clean the two you need for the show plate yourself, and Brianne can finish the rest once the smoke clears around five o'clock. You don't anticipate that they'll fly out the door, and for Raffy to clean a few orders à la minute, though terribly messy and disruptive, is doable if necessary. So Brie can get to them when she has the chance.

The only things left are the pasta and the terrine, but you trust that Stefan and Chef will take care of those dishes between the two of them, so you don't even allow yourself to think about them.

With the proteins covered, you can focus on the garnishes. They are relatively simple but require a fair amount of work. The "carrot" on the monk dish, for example, refers to a carrot puree. The process is less obvious than making baby food. You have to cook the carrots under a cartouche in bay-and-juniper-scented carrot juice, which means that someone has to juice some carrots and chop up others. The "endive" in that dish refers to a classically braised endive, but someone needs to halve them before they can be cooked. The beluga lentils are cooked, but they need to be inspected for quality. The tarragon needs to be picked for the compound butter, and the mise for the sapori forte needs to be cut. The potatoes need to be peeled and dressed. The potato dressing needs to be made. The boquerones sauce needs to be made. Herbs need to be picked. The line needs to be set. The carrots need to be pureed — but they're not even cooked yet. They're not even cut yet. There is so much to do, too much to do.

You step outside to smoke a cigarette on the loading dock and figure out where your head is at.

When you return, the kitchen is abuzz with activity. New sounds can be heard: the whoosh of lighted burners, the splutter of fat in pans, the clank and bonk of steel on steel. All the rest of the line cooks have arrived. And they've all jumped right to action.

Raffy has gotten started on the evening's sauces. He's begun reducing wines, re-therming bouillons, toasting spices, finessing fats into emulsion. VinDog and Warren have taken down the stocks and are now starting to set their lines, buzzing purees and turning vegetables, respectively. Catalina whips creams, rinses greens, and slices salumi in her corner on the cold side. Julio, arms bloodied, continues carving away at thick slabs of meat, slicing portions from primal cuts. Everyone has multiple projects up and running and, like worker bees, they buzz away at them, quickly and quietly, as if to some inaudible universal rhythm.

Being surrounded by a whole crew of people hard at work is usually comforting, but today it's only superficially so. The specials have utterly consumed you, and as a result, you and Stefan have completely neglected the regular menu. The line cooks are here to handle that problem. They're here to work on their prep lists, which center on the everyday dishes, for which the mise en place must be done fresh daily. While they might be *capable* of helping you out with the specials, their focus must remain with à la carte.

What's more, the work that everyone else has started has eaten up valuable real estate on the stovetops and tables. It's cat and mouse now for burners and boards. People are beginning to get keyed up.

"Where the fuck are my third pans, Kiko?" squawks Raffy. "Every fucking day with this shit."

"Vete a la verga, puto. Aquí. Tomale."

"Whose rondeau is this on my flat-top?" says Vinny.

"My bad, dog," says Warren. "That's me."

"Yeah, well, do me a favor and shit up your own station," he says, shoving the rondeau onto Warren's side of the stove. "This thing is about to explode. Pay attention."

"Ladies, please," wails Julio. *"Mucha* blah blah blah. *Ustedes ya me están dando dolor de cabeza."*

All you can do is put your head down and cook, which is fine, because you do it well when you do it.

You're picking herbs for the plats du jour when out of the corner of your eye you spot Brianne. Her arrival means it's nearing 1500, which is unsettling, but it also means you now have a second set of hands to help pull you through.

"Yo, Brie, what up," you say, extending your hand for the shake. "Listen, as soon as you're ready I need you to hop right into a few special projects for me, yeah?"

"No problem, Chef," she says. "I'm about to change right now."

When she returns in her whites, you instruct her on how to cut and juice the carrots, and you tell her to bring them up in a pot when they're ready. You'll be able to keep an eye on them once they get on the stove, and they shouldn't take more than half an hour. As far as pureeing them goes, well, they'll be done when they're done. You also show Brianne how you want the endive cut and the potatoes peeled, both of which she should be able to finish by around 1600, once she's through with the carrots. The potato dressing will take you five minutes, so you are fine with pushing that to the bitter end. The braised endive will be a quick job, too, once the stove clears up. You can even set it to run into the beginning of service if you want, because endives don't take very long to cook and you can store them in their liquor by the stove's chimney once they've come up to temperature.

You've elbowed out some space on the flat-top for an *evasée* in which you've set some white wine and sweated shallots to reduce for the boquerones sauce, and you brought out some heavy cream, the butter, and the anchovies so you can toss them in directly when the wine has come down *à sec.* You've inspected the beluga lentils and certified that they are fit to be served, and you've located some good duck fat, which will be used to pick them up. You showed Julio the rig for the tarragon butter and he's agreed to take care of it before service starts.

"So do you think you can get it done by four-thirty?" you say.

"Do I look like an octopus?" he says.

"The butter's out, the tarragon's picked. It'll take you two seconds."

"It'll take *you* two seconds," he says.

"I'm not asking."

The only major project left is the mise for the sapori forte. There is plenty of time for you to set up a board and get it done. You've moved your station to the pass, where you can observe both sides of the line. It is cleaner there, and you adjust your setup to fit the atmosphere. Your fish blades have been replaced by a lone ten-inch Gyutou — "Excalibur," an old favorite — and your cutting board is smaller now. A quartet of two-quart Cambros flanks the board, and whole carrots and cornichons breeze beneath your knife from left to right, as with smooth strokes you convert the raw ingredients into usable food.

The afternoon is finally beginning to coalesce. You've pushed through the chaos, established a sense of control over it. You've hit your rhythm. You are getting it done. You've been so efficient, in fact, that you've even found time to throw in a quick pan of filberts to toast for Chef — garnish for the terrine, which he said he would take care of, from A to Z — assuming that he would appreciate your contribution to the dish. Your eyes still dart here and there every now and again, but you feel for once as if you are going to make it out in time. A feeling of comfort comes over you.

All of a sudden Chef's meaty hands come thundering down on your shoulders and the comfort goes to smash. Your knife slips a bit, nearly snipping a pinky tip.

"Talk to me, *papi*," he says. "Where are we at?"

"Looking good, Chef," you say.

"Ready by four-thirty?" he says.

"*Oui,* Chef," you say. "Always ready."

Getting There

Being there means being ready. When it comes to service, being ready means having everything in its place by the time the first order comes in. On days like today, when you have a hefty prep list to contend with, getting there can be difficult. The only way to do it is to get a good rhythm going.

A good rhythm is any method of working that promotes maximum productivity. The specific method will vary from task to task, but it always comprises some specific succession of steps — (a) followed by (b) followed by (c), etcetera — which you repeat over and over again.

For simple jobs, this might be how you use your hands:

(a) Left hand picks up pear
(b) Right hand peels pear
(c) Left hand places pear in acidulated water

For something like whole animal butchery, the rhythm might be the way you choreograph your cuts:

(a) Head
(b) Feet
(c) Wings
(d) Legs
(e) Thighs
(f) Oysters
(g) Breasts
(h) Tenders
(i) Pope's nose

For more complicated jobs, like *pommes fondant,* let's say, it's all about how you approach the project as a whole:

(a) Peel all potatoes
(b) Cut all potatoes into 5 × 25 mm coins
(c) Sear all potatoes on one side in rondeau
(d) Flip all potatoes
(e) Deglaze rondeau with veal stock
(f) Mount veal stock with butter
(g) Season with salt, pepper, and aromatics
(h) Remove all potatoes from rondeau
(i) Cool all potatoes in prechilled hotel pan

In all cases, you follow the sequence with precision. Not only does the repetition yield consistency, it also works to encourage speed. As your body acclimates to the motion, you naturally do it more quickly. You begin to move like a machine, without even having to think about it. And the less you have to think about it, the more brain space you have to look into the future. Like a skilled billiards player, you begin anticipating your next move and the one after that, so that when one task is done, you don't waste time trying to figure out what follows. You move seamlessly between activities, shaving precious seconds off the overall time it takes to complete your mise en place. Before you know it, you're scratching items off your prep list in droves.

Today your rhythm has been brilliant; you've been a paragon of efficiency. Chef threw a vicious curveball at you with all these complicated specials, but you've knocked it out of the park. It's 1600 now — an hour before service starts — and you are already almost there. You take a moment to recap what you've accomplished.

The carrots are done. After you pureed them you passed the substance through a *tamis* sieve and it came out smooth as silk, bright orange, absolutely scrumptious. It is the essence of carrot. The mustard dressing for the potatoes is done. You shaved just enough truffle into it. Truffle can be dangerous. Too much can be pungently overwhelming, but just enough can give the right dish an ineffable warmth. The boquerones sauce is done. It is not overly fishy, not overly creamy, not overly salty. The monkfish roulades are done. They are wrapped and sitting in the fish box. The endive is done. It is sitting in a hotel pan on the stove's piano, steeping in its braising liquid. The sapori forte is done. All its ingredients have been incorporated, with the exception of the tarragon butter, with which it will be mounted, à la minute, on the pickup. The agnolotti are done. The turnips are done. Basically everything is done. And you still have half an hour before the premeal staff meeting.

It's important to use this time wisely. All the food might be ready, but it still needs to be organized among the stations. Typically, a line cook won't fuss over mise en place for a special, because technically it's not his responsibility to do so, it's yours. You need to break the food down into a manageable storage format — quart containers and third pans are often best, because they don't take up much space on the station — and deliver it to him. Plates, too, need to be collected. Catalina will definitely be picking up the terrine off the garde manger station on a wooden board, Chef's standard approach to charcuterie. VinDog will pick up the agnolotti off meat entremet (which tends to double as the pasta station), and you can't imagine it would go in anything other than a bowl. Raffy will pick up the sardines and the monk off fish roast, probably on an oval and a large round respectively. Julio's got the pork, probably on large round as well.

When it comes time to pick up the show plates, Chef will demonstrate how everything is to be plated. He will not, however, give you much direction in the way of descriptions for the floor. You are expected to gather that information yourself. And since he hates talking to the people out front, you are expected to dispense it to the waitstaff as well.

Every new dish will prompt certain questions from the front of the house. You need to anticipate these questions and provide good answers.

Foreign words and obscure ingredients will come up straightaway. You need to know that *boudin blanc* is a white sausage made of ground pork, whole eggs, liver, milk, and pig hearts. You need to know that a squab is a pigeon. You need to know that confit means "preserve," and that the standard method of confiting savory foods is to slowly poach them in fat. You need to know that verjus means essentially "green juice," and that it is made from the juice of unripe grapes, and that even though it is very acidic, it is not technically a vinegar because it hasn't undergone the fermentation process that vinegar undergoes. You need to know that a filbert is a hazelnut. You need to know that rocket is arugula. You need to know that quince, also known as *marmelo* or *membrillo,* is a fruit not unlike an apple. You need to know that herring are native to the North Atlantic, and that they are small oily fish with immense nutritional value. They are rich in protein, vitamins D and B12, and omega-3 fatty acids, and, unlike their larger relatives, their heavy metal and contaminant toxicities are infinitesimal at best. You need to know that ramps are wild onions of incredible robustness from the Appalachian region of North America, which are available only in limited quantities for a very short amount of time beginning at the end of April, which is why we pickle them. You need to know that bo- querones are white anchovies cured in oil with garlic, parsley, and vinegar, and that they are far more palatable than their salty brown counterparts. You need to know that agnolotti are a sort of oblong ravioli originally from the Piedmont region of Italy, which are filled, in this case, with a mousse made of braised veal tongue, lemon thyme, and garlic confit. You need to know that the "winter" mushrooms in this pasta dish are girolles and velvet foots. You need to know that preserved lemon is lemon rind that has been pickled in lemon juice, salt, and sugar. You need to know that monkfish is an anglerfish from the northwest Atlantic. You need to know that foie gras, in this case, is the liver of a duck that has been specially fattened by way of the unlovely cornmeal gavage process. You need to know that beluga lentils are small, shiny black legumes. You need to know that endive, or chicory, is a bitter leaf vegetable from the daisy family. You need to know that black heritage pork is the meat of a large black European hog that is known for its special tenderness. You need to know that sous vide means "under vacuum" and describes the process of vacuum-sealing food in boilable plastic bags and slowly cooking them in a circulating water bath until they reach a highly specific internal temperature, so as to maximize texture and liquid retention. You need to know that the current law stipulates that pork must reach 145°F in order to destroy all vegetative forms of bacteria that might be naturally present in the meat. Cooking it sous vide allows you to regulate this with precision. You need to know that Tokyo turnips are baby turnips, similar in appearance to snow belle radishes. You need to know that guanciale is cured pig jowl from Umbria. You need to know that sapori forte means "strong flavors," and that the name refers to the piquancy of the ingredients — the cornichons, the mustard, the raisins, the tarragon — which, in combination, work to balance one another with strong results. You need to know about allergens. Gluten, lactose, tree nut, shellfish, and garlic intolerances are extremely common, but there are other sensitivities to bear in mind: orange, strawberry, persimmon, apple, pear, jackfruit, eggplant, corn, red meat, eggs, caffeine, alcohol, sulfites, sugar, salt, pepper. There are also religious restrictions, most commonly kosher and halal dietary law. You need to know everything about everything that's in every dish, and you must be able to identify which items may conflict with which dietary guidelines.

After you've figured out answers to the

standard questions, you need to decide how to endow your premeal note with some degree of panache. Servers are osmotic. The excitement you put into your presentation will drift into their presentations, which will in turn excite the diners and increase the likelihood that they will order one of the specials. Not only are specials a way to make money on in-house products that might otherwise have no outlet on the regular menu and therefore eventually become garbage, but they are also a way to develop new menu ideas and keep the atmosphere in the kitchen fresh and forward-looking. So you take care to include certain anecdotal material when explaining them.

For example, you might mention that quince is believed to have been the "golden apple" in the mythical garden of the Hesperides, known to grant its eaters eternal life; or that herring, one of the most salubrious fishes in the sea, has been part of human culture as long as written language, its consumption dating back to at least 3000 B.C.; or that the Cosby Ramp Festival, in Cosby, Tennessee — which takes place on the first weekend in May — invites thousands of people from all over the world to come and forage the "little stinkers" by hand; or that beluga lentils borrow their name from the beluga sturgeon, whose hard roe — the familiar beluga caviar — are similar in appearance to the legume; or that a girolle is a French chanterelle (which you'd think is a French term itself) and that velvet foots are wild enokitake mushrooms found on tree stumps in mulberry groves. You might share as much of this information as possible, so that the waitstaff can learn something. For the better of our servers, like Devon and Candice — the true professionals — this gesture will go a long way. They will absorb what you say and the energy with which you say it, and they will use it to sell more specials. For stooges like Rupert — the teenaged bungler who just came on board last week — your efforts may be in vain. But regardless of the extent to which they use or desire your presentation, it's important to give them all the information they could possibly need.

This is how you approach the last half hour before the premeal meeting, getting things in order, pondering. Once the mise en place is set, each dish can be prepared in five or ten minutes, sometimes even less, which means that you need to be on the line at 1620. It's quarter past now. Feeling confident about the shape you're in, you step outside to smoke a quick cigarette and rehearse your presentation.

Two drags in, Chef pops his head out the door.

"What the fuck?" he says. "You think you have time to smoke a cigarette right now? We're up in fifteen minutes. Are you even ready? Do you have the descriptions together?"

"Sorry, Chef. That's what I was out here —"

"Let's go!" he says. The door slams shut behind him. You smush the cherry off the cigarette on the sole of your shoe, save the remnants in your pack for later, and hustle inside after him.

Knowing that you guys will be doing the specials for the premeal note, the cooks have abandoned the line and taken seats elsewhere to break for a few minutes and be out of the way. The only people on the main stage are you, Stefan, and Chef. And Kiko, of course, is not far away, slowly making his way through the heaps of pots and pans that have accumulated over the course of the afternoon. His P.M. assistant hasn't shown up yet and his face is twisted over it.

Chef looks serious, too. He doesn't smoke — most experienced chefs don't because of the way it impacts the palate; it's something you need to work on quitting sooner rather than later — and even though he says it's okay for you to do so from time to time, you try never to let him see you do it. It is always bad when he has to fetch you from outside because he needs you and you are smoking. This particular occasion seems to have annoyed him thoroughly. Stefan can sense it as well. He raises his eyebrows, wrinkles his brow, avoids eye contact with you, keeps his head down, and just cooks. Everybody is quiet, intent. The air is hot and tense. It's Kiko who finally breaks the silence.

"*¿Que huele, güey? Huele como algo está quemando,*" he says.

Chef looks up, trains a stare on you, takes a suspicious whiff.

"Yeah, what is that?" he says.

Then it dawns on you. The filberts. You forgot to take them out.

"Ah, shit!" you say, and dash over to the oven.

Thick smoke billows out when you open the door. It smells carcinogenic and burns your eyes. You wave it away to reveal the pan of filberts. They're hammered.

"What is that?" Chef says again.

"It's filberts," you say. "I was toasting them up for you for the terrine."

"Why?" he says. "I already got them. I told you I had the terrine, A to Z. Was I unclear about that?"

"No, Chef."

"Come on, man, get it together," he says. "What's with you today?"

"Sorry, Chef."

"Get that shit out of here, it stinks."

"*Oui,* Chef."

You take the smoking pan to the back prep area. You shove on a faucet and toss the whole rig in the sink to cool it down. This is an important step, so that you don't burn a hole in the trash liner with the hot nuts. But your embarrassment has you acting a mite too aggressively, and when the pan hits the bottom of the bay, its handle smacks against the corner and cracks loose.

"God damn it," you say. "Can I get a break here?"

Without its handle, the pan is useless. You rinse the broken pieces in the cold water and toss them into the garbage.

Rogelio and Brianne are back there to witness this entire affair. They don't say anything, they only shake their heads. You can feel the humiliation in your cheeks.

"Aghh, whatever," you say.

All right, so you've left the samples out,

you've gotten caught smoking a cigarette, and now you've destroyed thirty dollars' worth of nuts and broken a hundred-fifty-dollar pan. Bad start. But, listen, enough of these bush league mistakes. It's time to get to business. It's time to take these specials to the hole.

When you return to the line, Chef is tossing the salad for the terrine and getting ready to go to plate. Stefan is bringing together the pan sauce for the agnolotti, mounting it with butter and fresh herbs. He has a bowl warming up under the salamander — hot food goes on hot plates.

"Hey, push that pasta back a minute, will you?" you call out.

"How long you need?"

"Five," you say.

"Five," he says.

"Five," Chef says.

The idea is to get to the pass with all the ingredients in no more than five minutes so that Chef can plate everything. You start setting pans about the flat-top to get hot. You throw down an oblong cast-iron Griswold for the monkfish and a stainless steel sauté pan for the pork. You coat the bottom of each with a thin skin of soya oil. The monkfish will take the longest, so that has to go down first. The rest of the garnish will

117

be picked up in one-quart saucepans, with the exception of the potato salad (which you dress quickly in a flat-bottomed bowl and set on the stove's piano near the fire to take the chill off). When the Griswold is hot, you season the monk and lay it in gently. There's a soft sizzle when the flesh touches the oil. The pork has already been fully thermalized in the circulator, so the cuisson is simple à la minute: a quick sear followed by a glace of pork jus. You cut the loin out of the bag and place it in the pan. Its own sizzle sings with the fish's.

Next is the garnish. You set up two of the saucepans on a wire rack toward the back of the flat-top. The rack is a flame tamer; the extra half inch it gives you diffuses the heat. This way you can warm things up without needing to tend to them as much. You ladle the sauces into those pans, boquerones in one, sapori forte in the other. Into another pan go the Tokyo turnips. They get a splash of stock, a dollop of soubise, a knob of butter, and a dash of salt. Into another pan go the lentils. They start with a spoon of duck fat and finish with stock and a knob of butter. Into another pan goes the pureed carrot. You whip it with a spoon to a fluffy consistency. Into another pan goes the endive. You bring it up to a simmer in the braising jus.

When all the pans are up and cooking, you lay a pair of herrings down on the plancha. They only take a couple of minutes.

You taste everything along the way for salt and pepper and acid. A sprinkle here, a dribble there, now a stir, now a shake.

You roll the pork to reveal a golden brown sear. You spin the monk and it's the same. It's pure science: when the surface of a piece of food reaches approximately 300°F, certain sugars in the food begin to react with certain amino acids in the food and they rearrange to produce a series of nitrogenous polymers and melanoidins, which are responsible for a variety of luscious flavors and aromas. It's called the Maillard reaction. When it happens before your eyes, though, it blows your hair back.

"Two minutes out," Chef says.

"Two," you and Stefan say back.

In order to bring the monkfish up to temperature quickly enough, you must baste it. The technique is called *arrosé*. You drop a knob of butter into the pan. As it melts, you begin to spoon it rapidly over the fish. Tilting the pan toward you so that the butter pools in the corner makes it easier. The heat and the motion of your spoon agitate the butter and it bubbles and browns. The major advantage of the technique is that you're effectively shrouding the fish on all sides with a blanket of bubbly brown butter, so that the flesh cooks not only where it is in contact with the pan, but all over its surface at the same time. It is a more delicate version of deep fat frying. The welcome side effect is that as the butter undergoes its own version of the Maillard reaction, it develops a rich nutty flavor, which impregnates the fish as you continue to baste. Adding a mashed garlic clove and fresh thyme enhances the flavor even more. Thus the fish cooks not just faster, but better. And since the technique works with meat as well as fish, you do it to the pork, too, for flavor's sake, alternating between the pans every five seconds or so.

After a minute, you check on them. Pork, like most land animals, seizes up as you cook it, so you can gauge its doneness by sight and touch. It should resist a poke of your finger in a certain familiar way. The monkfish, however, is a bit trickier. Since it's been heavily processed, it is very difficult to compute the effect that the heat has had on the inside by sight and touch alone. And since there is uncured foie gras on the inside, you need to be certain it's cooked all the way through.

The way you do this is with a cake tester, a thin metal pin about the length of a pencil. You insert the cake tester into the center of the fish and hold it there for ten seconds. When you remove it, you place it directly against the underside of your lower lip. If it is warm, the food is done. This technique has been around for hundreds of years, and it has a provincial flair to it, but it happens to be complexly scientific as well. The temperature at which most bacteria die, and at which protein begins to denature in such a way that it becomes cooked, is approximately 130°F. The temperature at which human skin begins to detect contact with heat is roughly 120°F. Empirical evidence suggests that a steel pin will, on average, undergo a ten-degree temperature decline in the time it takes to transfer it by hand from the interior of a cooked product to your lower lip. Ergo, when the cake tester is warm on your lip, the monkfish is thoroughly cooked.

"You there?" Chef says.

"*Oui,* Chef," you say.

You remove the meat and the fish from the heat and set them on a small steel drop tray, lined with a C-fold towel, to rest. All meat needs to rest before serving, so that the juices can redistribute themselves throughout the interior of the flesh. Usually fish is the opposite. It should be served immediately, otherwise valuable juices will leach out and the cut will dry up. Monkfish is a strange exception that takes kindly to resting. Herring are oily enough that the difference is negligible in this context. You slide the tray onto the pass for Chef.

Now it's time to put the finishing touches on all the garnishes. You taste everything one last time for seasoning and temperature and consistency and then slide them onto the pass one by one as well. The lentils and turnips and potatoes get another fold or two; the carrots get one more whip; the boquerones sauce gets one last stir. The sapori forte gets mounted with the tarragon compound butter — but only at the very last minute. The butter is there for two reasons: it flavors the sauce and it brings it together. It's science again. As the butter melts, its milk solids interact with the protein in the stock with which the sauce was made to become emulsifying agents. These surfactants, as they're called, are attracted to both water and oil, so they coat the oil molecules in the butter fat, allowing them to suspend homogenously within the water molecules in the stock. This gives the sauce an attractive consistency and a glassy luster. But you do this last because buttered sauces become unstable quickly, and too much heat can cause the fat to break out of emulsion, which is ruinous. Also, if you put it in too early, the chlorophyll in the tarragon will denature and become brown and unattractive. Chef hates it when herbs go "doo-doo brown. They're supposed to steep gently, like tea," he always says.

"To the plate?" Chef says.

"*Oui,* Chef," you say, sliding the rest of your garnish onto the pass.

Watching Chef plate things is inspirational. He makes artwork with a flourish of the spoon. It's as though he were born to arrange food on a plate.

There is an inherent beauty to the agnolotti, which call for little intervention. The thumb-size parcels have that imperfect quality unique to handmade things, which gives the dish an inviting charisma and precludes the need for ornamentation. The shimmer of the butter glaze is enough. Chef simply gives it a fold in the pan, spills it into a bowl, and flecks the dish with *fines herbes* and freshly cracked pepper.

The boudin blanc and squab confit concoction is a bit more of a composition. There is a certain amount of guesswork in the making of any terrine. Like the printmaker who can't tell exactly what his first proof will look like until he peels back the paper, a chef can never quite picture his terrine until he cuts it open. A smooth stroke of Chef's Sujihiki shows us that this one was a success — its cross-section is, as hoped, a kaleidoscopic array of colors and shapes. In order to accentuate this visual dynamism, Chef fashions the rest of the plate in geometrics. He places a carefully squared slice of the terrine on the left-hand side of an oblong board. Beside that goes the quince. He's poached the quince in white wine with clove and vanilla bean and blended the lot into a velvety puree, which he's able to quenelle, with a wave of the spoon, into the perfect prolate spheroid, a fragrant football of fruit on the board. Next to the quince goes a stack of ficelle toast points, which, when cut a certain way, recall parallelograms. At the far right he rests a bundle of arugula leaves, which add a feathery, peppery element to the arrangement. To finish, he scatters a few hemispheres of hazelnut and dots a few orbs of verjus fluid gel about the board.

The herring dish is similarly artistic in construction. It starts with the boquerones sauce, a film of which Chef spoons down the center of an oval plate. Next come the potatoes. He's ordered you to halve them across their short axis so that they don't roll around when he puts them down. He stands them upright about the plate, seemingly at random. Next are the ramps, which he distributes adventitiously as well. And finally the herring, which he lays nearly (but not quite) parallel to each other, just off the center of the plate. A dusting of smoked paprika and some torn celery leaves finish the dish. When it's done it looks like a field of Greek ruins through which a pair of beautiful fish have decided by chance to swim.

The pork dish has a more bucolic appeal. The meat is a hearty slab and the sauce is chunky with ingredients, which give it the look of a stew or *sugo.* Chef starts with the sauce again. This time he's a bit more scattershot with its application, drizzling it about in broad swooshes. Then come the turnips, laid here and there. The soubise cloaks them like cream, and in places the white sauce is allowed to drip a bit into the sapori forte. The droplets look like tiny pearls in a sea of other jewels. Now for the protein. Chef cuts a two-inch hunk off the end of the seared loin. The gentle nature of the sous vide process has lent the pork a special tenderness — the typically dry white meat is an even, rosy tone throughout, with a sheen of juices seeping up to the surface. He places it dead center on the plate to showcase the cut's stark brawn. Sliced chestnuts and freshly snipped tarragon leaves finish it off.

Finally there is the monkfish — a stupendous picture. It starts with a gob of carrot puree, dragged across the plate with the bottom side of a small offset spatula. The result is a cadmium orange swatch that looks more like oil paint than food. After that come the lentils, which he arranges in patches like shiny black moss on a forest floor. Then, with a pair of forceps, the endive goes down, its sharp cowlick of leaves saluting the sky. And then, finally, comes the fish. He cuts the shaft into four identical coins and shingles them down the center of the plate. As he does this, you notice that inside the roulade the foie gras has gone molten, which means you've cooked it perfectly.

"Nice job on the fish, guy," he says. "Exactly what I'm looking for."

"*Oui,* Chef," you say. Pride wells up in you.

He dabs a few drops of *sauce rôti* here and there. A couple of *pluches* of fresh dill, and the dish is complete.

"All right, let's do this," he says, and you

and he and Stefan grab all the plates and head out to the dining room.

Out front all the floor staff have joined forces preparing the restaurant for guests. Servers stage out silverware sets and pyramid-fold serviettes, while back waiters steam-press linens and allocate centerpieces. Bartenders slice citrus wedges and channel out twists, while their bar backs stock the low-boys with bottles and fill the speed rack kits with mixes. Maître d's and hostesses comb through the reservation books to determine when the big pushes are and which VIPs are coming when. Managers vet floral arrangements and scrutinize the cleanliness of everything.

Chef's presence captures everyone's attention when he enters. *"Achtung, malakas,"* he booms authoritatively. All activity stops. He sashays into the middle of the room, you and Stefan in tow, and begins disposing the plates about a large central table. "Time to eat," he says.

The staff hastily gather around, elbowing past each other for prime places at the table. Save perhaps for a shift drink at the end of the night, this is the highlight of their evening — a complimentary taste of the restaurant's most special offerings, prepared by none other than Chef himself. And everyone wants as much as they can get.

When stillness has settled over the throng, Chef folds his arms across his chest and gives you a nod. This is your cue.

"All right, guys," you say, clearing a frog or two from your throat. "Let's start with the appetizers. First up, we have a lovely terrine of boudin blanc and squab confit, served with rocket, filbert, quince, and verjus."

Uncertain hands spring into the air immediately. This is always annoying. *Just let me finish,* you think.

"Ahem. Boudin blanc," you continue, "in case you didn't know, is a French term meaning . . ."

BREAK

Relief always accompanies reentry into the kitchen after the premeal note. Even if you've nailed your specials presentation, which you usually do, it feels good to be back in your own atmosphere, where only a few people ask you questions and almost no one's eyes are on you.

You gently place the licked-clean plates in the dish area for Kiko, making sure they're not in danger of being broken, and join Chef at the pass.

"See, now we take a break," he says. "When the work is done. Go ahead and smoke your stupid cigarettes. Just make sure this pass is set before service."

This little respite is the equivalent of your lunch break. Ten cool minutes before service starts.

"Thanks, Chef," you say.

"When are you going to quit that shit anyways?" he says.

"Soon, Chef," you say.

Down the back corridor, you shove open the door to the loading dock, and the last remnants of afternoon sun spill in. You raise a hand to the sky and wait for your eyes to adjust to the glare of daylight in the shade of your fingers. You close your eyes and tilt your head back and allow the sun to filter its red blanket through your eyelids. When your vision has come to, you take a seat on a shady patch of curb and fire up a smoke.

December has done something ugly to the Village. A crust of salt cakes the pavement; slush mucks up gutters; cars and trucks splash winter's dirty porridge from potholes as they pass. People, bundled up like sausages, slip and shimmy in galoshes across frozen sidewalks up and down Sixth Avenue. You can see them from your perch, fifty paces down the alleylike side street. They don't notice you, but you notice them. They are getting off work, getting ready to start their weekends. Some of them are on their way out to eat or to a bar for happy hour. Others rush to the train station, on their way out of town for a couple of days to go skiing. Still others are tourists, just visiting for the weekend. They're here to Christmas shop. They're here to see the tree at Rock Center. They're suspiciously rosy-cheeked and healthy looking despite the wintry weather. It's been years since you've had anything that resembles a vacation. You look down at your grayish naked arms. You look up and down the block. There are other cooks and chefs tucked in clusters here and there, resting on other curbs and fire hydrants, in the shadows of other back doors. Their houndstooth pants give them away. They, too, are pale and smoking — chain-smoking, trying to suck down as many as they can before service starts. They, too, observe the passersby. None of the passersby seem to notice any of them, either.

You fire up another smoke.

You check your cell phone for the first time all day. A text from Vera, your girlfriend, time-stamped at 1500, says that she's going to stop by on your break to say hello. THAT'S COOL YEAH? she says. She knows the rig: you can't answer your phone when you're working. She understands. She works in the industry, too, at a smaller restaurant up the block. It's how you got together in the first place, and part of the reason you've managed to stay together these eighteen months: you run in the same crowds, you speak the same language, you understand each other's situation. She doesn't cook, though, she works the floor. But on the days she works, she passes by on her way in to see you quickly before service starts.

It's 1649 now; she should be here any minute.

The kitchen door swings open and Stefan saunters out. He sits down beside you on the curb and stretches his wiry legs out over the slush in the gutter. His eyes are no longer bloodshot. There's life in his face now. He's sweated out the toxins. He is human again. He lights up a cigarette, sends a gust of smoke skyward.

"So . . ." he says, taking another pull. "Your boy Raffy? He don't look too hot. He's banged *out,* guy."

"Oh?" you say.

"Yeah, he just hurled in the sink out back."

"Man."

"I thought I'd take the opportunity to step out and enjoy a quick fag. Probably the last one I'll get the rest of the night. We're up near three hundred, you know."

You pull on your smoke, look down the street, exhale through your nose.

"Seriously," he says. "Chef just told me to ramp up the par on the agnolotti to fifty. I'll be back there another hour rolling that shit out."

"Las risas no tienen límite," you say.

"Anyways, listen," he says, sucking in one

132

last deep drag of smoke and rocketing the butt a great distance into the street. "I'm going back in. It's probably not a good idea for you to be out here too much longer, either, the way you're rolling today. You don't want to piss Chef off any more than you already have."

"I know, I know," you say. "I'm just gonna say what's up to V."

"All right, I'm gonna go crank a yam while the bathroom is still clean," he says. "I gotta shit like a Clydesdale right now. Then I'm back on pasta. Let me know if you need help setting up the pass."

Just then, you spot Vera down the block, rounding the corner of Sixth Avenue. You could pick her out a mile away. The way strands of her loosely knotted yellow hair flit in the wind behind her. The way she's shaped, with a crane's frame, long and taut. The way she carries herself, milky like a dancer, from a childhood in ballet followed by a decade of chasséing through dining rooms.

With a pair of degrees (in theater and art therapy), Vera could do much more than wait tables if she wanted to. But she keeps on in the industry because it's quick, mindless money — seven or eight hundred dollars cash for three or four drowsy nights —

and it allows her a lot of free time to do as she pleases. It's a power move on her part, the smart choice, and she knows it.

"There's my girl," you say to yourself. She signals you with a tiny wave of the hand.

Stefan notices her on his way in and waves back with sham cheer.

"Three hundred tonight, Vera, how 'bout that!" he yells down. "Yeah. Fuck my life," he grumbles, flipping the door open and ducking back inside.

"What's up, baby," she says, planting a juicy one on your lips. "Having a little smoky treat?"

"*You* know, baby," you say with an exhale. "Same shit."

You pull her in to you. Her hair smells of the yuzu shampoo she uses. She says you always smell of garlic. Right now you know you smell of cigarettes. She hates the smell on you, but she understands that they're your way out when you're at work, they're your escape. Your cigarette is burned down to the filter. You flick it away. Never have you wanted to quit more than you do right now.

You twist your limbs with hers like loose shoelaces. The skin of her hands is silken beneath your calloused fingers. For just this very moment you begin to forget about the burned hazelnuts and the monkfish roulades. You lean together against the hood of a parked car looking back toward Sixth.

"So, three hundred covers?" she says.

You don't want to talk about numbers. You kiss her on the soft bottom part of her earlobe. You press your philtrum to the familiar freckle on her thumb; exhale.

"Yeah," you say. "But I should still be able to get out around ten o'clock. Wanna meet up and grab some drinks with me afterward?"

"Ten o'clock?" she says. "Really?"

"Yeah," you say. "I opened today, babe. I've been here since nine, remember."

"Yeah, but that doesn't mean —"

Just then, the kitchen door flies open and a trio of back waiters storms out, led by a noticeably consternated Hussein. They are all carrying empty plates, heading straight for you and Vera. The two of you rise to meet them.

"Chef," Hussein says. "We need to talk."

"Yes, Hussein?"

"It's almost five o'clock and still no family meal," he says, brandishing the empty plate for dramatic effect. All this work on the specials has distracted you from one of the essential daily tasks: staff meal.

You steal an apologetic look at Vera.

"Hussein, can't you see I'm in the middle of someth—"

"We pay for this, Chef," he says. "It comes out of our paycheck, you know."

"I know, Hussein, I know. Is there literally nothing?"

"Rice and bean," he says. "No meat, no vegetable. Only rice and bean. We cannot live on rice and bean. We are supposed to have fish and vegetable, too."

"You ask any of the cooks? Julio? Juan?"

"They say talk to you," he says. "They say you are boss."

You instinctively pull out another smoke and fire it up. You cast a glance across the street and lock eyes with a cook who has been out smoking this whole time. He smiles and shakes his head in acknowledgment.

"Okay, Hussein. Listen," you say. Your tone is professional, clean. "It's been a very busy afternoon —"

"Busy? I'm busy, too! And you! Outside smoking cigarette!" His voice is getting louder, more confrontational. The other back waiters stare wooden-faced at you. Vera averts her eyes, looks down the block. You sigh.

"Listen, Huss—"

"We need to eat! It comes out of our

paycheck!"

The insolence reaches its crescendo and the two other back waiters inch forward menacingly. Vera backpedals a step or two, just enough for you to notice. A switch flips in you.

"All right, enough!" you say. "I understand your dilemma, and I apologize. Nobody means any disrespect. It has been a very busy afternoon and we simply haven't had *time* to prepare an abundant staff meal. But I assure you, you will not starve. Somebody will fix you something more to eat before the night is out. Until then you're going to have to be patient and show some fucking respect!"

Hussein lets go an exaggerated sigh. "It better!" he says, and the three storm back into the kitchen, the door slamming behind them.

You look at your watch: 1700 on the nose.

"It looks like you need to get back in there, huh, babe?" Vera says, eyes cast downward.

You look up and down the block. The cook from across the street has vanished. It's already begun for him, you imagine. He's in the paint, running around inside, starting to sweat. Lifting and flipping, searing and sizzling. Suddenly all three hundred

137

of tonight's covers begin to creep back into your consciousness. And now staff meal is a bust. Friday night is about to get real.

"Yeah, I gotta go," you say.

"It's cool," she says. "I just wanted to say hi. I have to get to work myself." She gives you one more long kiss on the lips. "Just give me a buzz when you get out and we'll see what we can do about those drinks."

"I love you, Vera," you say.

"I love you, too, sweet pea," she says.

"Thanks for coming to see me," you say.

She winks and takes off.

Watching her leave, you're taken anew by her grace. How deftly she negotiates the wedge that is your work. Right then you begin to wonder how stupid you must look, standing alone in the cold with nothing but this chef's outfit on.

This sucks, you think.

You chuck your butt into the slush and duck back into the kitchen.

Every day, when the clock strikes five, excitement takes you. It's a feeling in your belly that tickles you and jumps around: the awareness that something significant is about to happen, the upshot of which is only marginally predictable.

For the line cooks, this sensation is often

very uncomfortable, because it's usually accompanied by a fierce sense of doom. Every line cook secretly wonders whether he has enough mise en place for the night; he worries that he might not. He wonders which station will get hit the hardest; will it be his? There is no telling what the guests will favor on any given night, and on the chance that the orders are lopsided to one side or the other, the line cook on the victim station could be in serious trouble. When it's busy, sometimes you run out of things. Whole chickens, beef skirts, specials — it's impossible to purchase perfectly all the time. But running short on *prep* is unacceptable. To eighty-six a menu item for lack of proper foresight during the day is a radical violation of kitchen dogma. People have lost their jobs for less. And cooks all bear this in mind the closer it gets to showtime. *Do I have enough backup?* they wonder. *Is there time to make more?*

For the sous chefs and chef, it's different. The day for you is like dragging a toboggan up to the top of the hill — once it's there, you sit back and let it ride.

You put on a crisp jacket and a fresh apron, gather some side-towels, and begin to ready the pass.

Just as in any other section, there is a place

for everything on the pass, and everything is to remain in its place. All the surfaces must be spotlessly clean, and everything must be neat and organized. While cleanliness and order are the watchwords for all areas of the kitchen, it is especially important to live by them at the pass, because everything that leaves the kitchen does so by way of the pass. It is the food's last contact with the kitchen. Everything that arrives at it or issues from it must be perfect, so it must be perfect, too.

You mop it down with sanitizing water, squeegee it clean, and buff it dry with a clean towel. You turn on the telescoping heat lamps and retract them to their highest position. You check the snipped herbs and garnishes for quality. You make sure the pepper mill is full. You make sure there are plenty of spoons.

You're neatly folding the side-towels when Chef makes his approach. You can feel his presence behind you. He's taping up the seating forecast — a bar graph spat out by the reservationist's software that predicts the big pushes in fifteen-minute chunks — and a copy of the menu.

"We're up around three hundred," he says. "But it's all pushed to the second seating. Check it out."

He directs your attention to the eight o'clock region on the graph, where the bars are extremely tall. Beginning at eight, you will do nearly thirty covers every half hour for three hours. This translates to approximately one hundred eighty plates of appetizer, one hundred eighty plates of entrée, and about one hundred twenty plates of dessert, give or take, all passing through your hands over the course of about two hundred minutes.

"Madness," you say.

"Yeah," he says. "Fucking massacre."

You almost want to hide the news from the cooks. They're already worried enough.

"Listen," Chef says. "How are we looking? We got spoons? Towels? The whole rig, yeah?"

"*Oui,* Chef. Everything."

"All right, then," he says. "Why don't you roll me up some tampons. I'll take the pass if anything comes in. Party don't start for a few anyways."

"*Oui,* Chef," you say.

By "tampons" he means plate wipes — lengths of cheesecloth that have been rolled up into tight, finger-size bundles and sprayed lightly with an alcohol solution, meant to clean, degrease, and sanitize the plates. They are the perfect size and shape

141

for moving nimbly around rims, removing any errant drips or spatters without touching any of the food. Towels and napkins tend to be too cumbersome for this kind of detail work. The wipes just happen to look like tampons.

As you're rolling them up, you notice that the line has gone suspiciously quiet. Quiet like the inside of a soldiers' boat bound for Omaha Beach. The cooks have finished stocking their stations and now they're arranging the finishing touches on their mise en place, slicing, chopping, turning, worrying. You feel compelled to march around and inspect their work.

You can tell a lot about a cook by the state of his station just prior to service. If it is neat and well organized you know he is in good shape. You can see he's had the self-control to work clean to begin with, the discipline to put right any messes he's made in the process, and the agility and efficiency to complete all his projects on schedule, while still leaving time to codify his workspace. That his station is free of clutter also suggests he has the mental clarity required to accommodate whatever toil service holds for him. In short, a clean station allows you to assume that a cook is ready, that he is *there*.

A dirty station, however, paints an ominous picture. If a cook hasn't had a chance to stop and regroup — to change out his board, to wipe down the tabletop, to refresh his spoon water — you know he is in a bad way. You know he probably still has a lot of work to do, which means he might not be ready by the time the first order comes in. And if he's not ready when the first order comes in, there's a chance he never will be. He'll be playing catch-up all night and he might go down in flames.

Fortunately for us, Warren and VinDog are completely dialed in. Their stations are ultratight and well supplied: towels folded, surfaces spotless, saltshakers, pepper mills, and fat and acid bottles full to the brim — their mise is truly en place. But no matter how nice things look on the surface, as their sous chef you still need to ask the question.

"Big night tonight, Don Juan," you say sternly. "Are you ready to roll?"

"*Oui,* Chef," Warren says. "Always ready."

"What about you, VinDog? You going to be able to handle this push?"

"*Tu sabes,*" he says. "Never scared."

They're so accustomed to being busy on the station that getting there, for them, is the easy part. You just give them the number and they will get done whatever they need to do in order to be prepared. Their ability to accommodate these massive numbers has yet to be determined, but they will certainly have all the mise en place they need for it.

Garde manger is also fully set. Catalina is rock-steady there. She's been cooking almost as long as you've been alive. She is never unprepared. She always overpreps in large batches. It's not the ideal way of going about it, but you know as well as she does that she's always thinking a day or two out, so she's always ready for even the busiest night. And her station is never, *ever* messy.

"¿Que onda, gringo?" she says with familiar braggadocio, as you look over her rig.

"Nada," you say. *"Sólo digo hola."*

Julio is there as well. His first round of meats have been pulled out to temper, his sous vide baths are rolling at retherm temperatures, and his squeaky-clean cutting board awaits cooked cuts for slicing. As usual, his face is stoically emotionless. But he does express some concerns about the reservationist.

"What's with the second seating?" he says. "Who booked that shit?"

"I know," you say, checking the temperature on the pork in the circulator. "It's gonna get ugly. Can you handle it, baby?"

"We shall see," he says.

This brings you around to Raffy on fish roast. Unlike the rest of the cooks, his station seems uncommonly sloppy. It's not dirty, it's not terribly disorganized, it's not even understocked. It's just not tight. He usually has a fresh box of gloves on the station; the box he's got now is half empty. He usually has a stack of C-folds; now there are none in sight. He usually folds his side-towels meticulously; now they're in a heap. The bag in his slim-jim is askew; his spoon water is dirty; his pepper mill is nowhere to be found. His station looks the way it usually does midway through service. But we haven't even started yet. It's uncharacteristic in an unsettling way. You expect more of him. Your brow furrows.

"Everything all right, guy?" you ask.

"Yeah, I'm cool," he says. "Everything is cool."

His face is pasty and beaded with sweat. His eyes dart around. He seems to be busy trying to look busy, instead of actually accomplishing work — he's boondoggling.

"But, hey, my printer's running low on ink," he says. "I can barely read the dupes. Could you hook me up with another cartridge?"

To make life easier for the cooks, every section has its own ticket printer. This way they don't need to rely on memory alone when a multitude of orders rushes in. Nor do they have to fetch duplicate copies from Chef when a table is flagged with special instructions — the tickets are right in front of them. The trade-off is, the cooks themselves are responsible for ensuring they have the requisite paper and ink. You make an exception and head toward the office to fetch a backup for Raffy.

You find Chef in there, bent under the desk, grabbing a cartridge for you. He spied your interaction with Raffy like a predator.

"Your boy don't look too hot," he says, tossing you the ink.

"I know," you say.

"Brew flu?" Chef says.

"Definitely the brew flu," you say.

"Listen," Chef says. "I want you to keep an eye on him. If he doesn't snap out of it in the next hour, he's gonna go down in flames when the push hits. And you're gonna be the one to dig him out when he's in the shits."

"*Oui,* Chef," you say.

"Good. Let's boogie."

Back on fish roast, Raffy's got the shakes. He's drinking water now. He can't keep it together. Your hands are steady as you load the ink into his printer.

"Listen," you say, calmly. "What's your deal?"

"What do you mean?" he says. "Oh, you mean the sink. Yeah, no, it's cool. I cleaned it up. I'm cool. Just something I ate or something. Fucking street meat."

"Can you do the job?" you say, soberly.

"Yeah, I'll be fine," he says.

You're pretty sure you can't trust this response. But the alternative is sending him home, which means you would have to work the station. This is not an attractive alternative because, simply put, working a station is hard. The pass is much easier. There is less sweating on the pass, less bending and lifting. There is less fire. Plus, you get to practice your plating skills on the pass, which is not only enjoyable but also crucial for your development. No matter how much you love cooking, working the pass on a busy night is almost always preferable.

So since Raffy is not actually asking to go home, which is usually what the hungover cook will do when he sees a way out, you figure the best bet is just to see what happens. Sometimes vomiting makes you feel better when you're hungover. Maybe he pulled the trigger intentionally. Maybe he'll be better in an hour, after he's sweated a bit.

You finish installing the cartridge and slap down the printer's lid. As the plastic snaps shut, a ticket begins to emerge, as though your filling it with ink were the cause. You look around. The printers on the other sections begin to activate as well. A mechanical buzzing fills the kitchen.

It is the first order of the night.

All heads cock silently toward Chef, awaiting direction.

"Ordering . . ." he says. "Four-top. First course: two agno, one white asparagus, one terrine, and a crudo. Followed by: one pork, one skate, one gnocchi, and a monkfish."

"*Oui,* Chef!" everyone exclaims.

"You sure you can handle it?" you ask Raffy.

"I got it, man," he says.

You clap him on the shoulder and join Chef at the pass.

Stefan is there in a moment as well.

"How was the shit, guy?" you ask him.

"Radioactive, bro," he says, tying the strings on a crisp new apron.

SERVICE

It is our first thought in the morning; it is on our minds when we lie down to sleep. It's what we spend our days preparing for; it's the focus of our evenings. *Service:* the work of a servant; an act of help or assistance; employment in or performance of work for another; an organized system of labor used to supply the needs of the public; the act or manner of serving food and drink to guests. Food service. This is our industry.

Service in a restaurant begins the moment the doors open to customers. For our purposes, this happens at 1700. All that came before and all that's yet to come matters only insofar as it influences the flow of service. Prep work matters. Attendance matters. Readiness matters. Inventory matters. Purchasing and receiving matter. Trifling arguments, hangovers, résumés, relationships, feelings, what happened at the bar last night, and what your trip in this morning was like — these things cease to mean anything once the first order reaches the kitchen.

In the beginning there is the first seating, the first two hours, in which we hope to fill every seat in the house at least once, hope to do a "full turn." But things usually come soft in the first seating. It's easy, relaxed. Whereas a midservice pickup may entail making food for six, seven, eight tables simultaneously, first-seating pickups are often only two or three tickets at a time. Sometimes you can even afford to go table by table, one by one.

Five o'clock is too early for people on Friday. The customers you get at this hour order light. They're coming from work, taking late business lunches with colleagues, stopping by for drinks and a quick bite, no frills. Or else they're the pretheater crowd: large, mussed-up troupes on budgets and timetables. Their numbers are big sometimes, but they always have someplace else to be and it shows: single-course meals, often forgoing entrées altogether. Entrées take too long for the stoppers-by. So in the first seating you get a bunch of easy tickets — duck soup here, apple pie there.

As a result, the cooks remain unruffled. They are like tennis players during the first game in a three-set match. They catch up on prep, crack jokes, get a groove going. There is still plenty of time to do things right, plenty of time before things get crazy.

According to the seating forecast, we won't finish our first full turn until at least 1930. Yet Chef, aware of what a challenge the second seating presents, aware of how quickly things can spin out of control, aware of how important a flawless first seating is, stands poised at the pass. His back is straight, his legs are spread wide, almost obscenely so. He stands this way to minimize lumbar fatigue. When your legs are shoulder width apart or better, you don't need to hunch your back in order to reach the things on the table. Your center of gravity is lowered. Your hands and eyes are closer to your work. But Chef also stands this way for logistical purposes. A wide posture prevents others from getting too close to his work, keeps them out of his light, keeps them from lousing up his fine touch with snipped herbs and spice dusts.

He's flanked on his right and left by you and Stefan, respectively. You're his wing-men, each responsible for one half of the brigade. Stefan receives food from the meat side, you take the fish. Your job, as the hot pans flock to the pass, is to taste the cooks' work for seasoning, texture, and temperature. You are quality control. You taste all of it. If the fluke is cold, you send it back; if the pommes purees are lumpy, you send them back; if the sauce has a skin, if the soubise needs salt, if the turnips are hammered, you send them back.

You do this, first, so that Chef doesn't have to. He has other things to do. Not only does he have to plate almost everything, but he also has to expedite, which is to say manage the tickets, group the pickups, control the flow. Plus, when *you* send a pan of food back to a cook, you have the power in you to keep it under wraps, make light of it. You are capable of doing it nicely, unconcernedly. Chef? No. His temper is incendiary. Allowing something imperfect to reach his hands might set him off, and the shrapnel hits everybody when he blows.

The other, more important reason you taste things and send them back to cooks is so that guests don't have to. Not so much because a guest's opinion matters — many people have an opinion about the way things should be cooked, but few understand what the best way is and why — but because food that comes back after it's gone out to the dining room is incredibly disruptive. It breaks up the flow.

152

We call anything that returns to the kitchen a refire, because usually it returns to the stove or the oven. It's not the right doneness, it needs more time. It needs to go back into the fire. What really happens to it, though, is it goes into a sort of purgatory. Its mates have already reached the table, they're already being eaten. The cook who originally prepared it is on to the next pickup, he's stabbed the ticket, he can't remember what the order even was. Yet here it is, this rogue plate of food. And now the cook has to stop what he's doing to figure it out — quickly. If it's a piece of meat (which is unlikely, given Julio's aptitude with temperatures), perhaps it can be salvaged by a turn or two on the grill or in the oven. But suppose it's been *over*cooked. Or suppose the customer's cut it to bits and it's unplateable now. Or suppose it's a piece of fish (forget it — fish can never be salvaged). In this case, he has no choice but to start the mental process of the dish all over: find the ticket, decrypt it, fire a new piece of the appropriate protein, throw down new pans for the appropriate vegetables, heat a new portion of sauce. He's welcome to hasten the process by using another of the same cut that he's already got working for a different table, but doing that will in turn slow down that pickup. Not to mention the unfavorable effect this process will have on the current pickup. Because he's already begun working on something else, which he's stopped to address the refire. He's now got two minutes left to pick up the current table, yet he finds himself somehow working on a table from the past, and in so doing, complicating the tables of the future. The present moment is gone. Refires get gnarly in a flash. Which is why you, the sous chef, must make sure everything is perfectly cooked before you pass it on to Chef for plating.

But your job is more involved than simply tasting food.

When a server punches a table's order into the restaurant's Point of Sale system — the POS — all food purchases get routed by the computer to the kitchen in the form of a ticket, or "dupe," which prints out in full on the central printer located at the pass. Chef plucks these tickets from the printer, decrypts their various built-in codes (table number, food order, order number, time stamp, seating assignments, guest count, course lines, special instructions, server's name), and arranges them, based on what they call for, in chronological order on the "board." The board is a metal ticket rack located at the pass, which not only holds the tickets in place so they don't blow away, but also acts as an organizing post. Meanwhile, at the very same time, abridged versions of each ticket print out on each of the sections. The cooks similarly decrypt them and hang them on their own ticket racks.

A given order may call for several dishes, but the POS is programmed in such a way that the dupe that each respective station receives lists only those items required of that station. This enables the cooks to isolate their responsibilities without having to sift through a half dozen other items. But since Julio can't see what Raffy has on board, and vice versa, it's important that upon receipt of the order, Chef read out to everybody what has come in. This way, Raffy won't start a piece of fish that takes five minutes if he knows it's going with a steak that takes ten, and neither of them will start anything if the table has ordered loads of appetizers for Catalina.

Chef will start by saying "Ordering . . ." which gathers everyone's attention. To flag the announcement with the word "ordering" is important because it allows the busy cook to distinguish unrelated or unimportant line chatter from new responsibilities — actual ordering. People need to communicate, and often that communication between linesmen involves the rereading of tickets to each other. But a seasoned cook knows not to begin making anything new until he hears *Chef* call the order.

"First course," he will say, reading out the appetizers, "followed by" midcourses and entrées, and occasionally desserts. When he's done calling the ticket we all say "*Oui,* Chef." We do so in unison. The call back itself is a confirmation that the order has been heard; that we perform the call back in unison is a confirmation that we are all working at the same tempo, dancing to the same rhythm. In the best kitchens, the "*Oui,* Chefs," loud and clear, seem to issue from one single, machinelike creature.

These "followed by" items Chef mentions are considered to be "on board," meaning "to be made later." Items that require a long time to cook might be started right when the ticket comes in. For quicker preparations, a cook may not start the work until the server punches in a "fire" ticket. When something is fired, we begin the final stages, the last couple of minutes of work. For a goose that has been roasted in advance, to fire it may be to cut the meat off the bone and crisp its skin under the salamander. For a skate wing that cooks very rapidly, to fire it is to put it in the pan.

If a table hasn't ordered appetizers for some reason, Chef will start by saying "Order fire . . ." meaning "make this immediately." If they're in a hurry, we'll make it "on the fly." If they *have* ordered appetizers, but they're eating slowly — suppose they are a couple on a date, and they're spending more time looking deep into each other's eyes than they are digging deep into their food — they get "pushed back," literally to the back of the line of tickets on the board, and we "hold fire" until the server notifies us that the table is ready.

Ideally, tables with multiple courses should be punched in as a single unit, with each course separated from the next by a course line. The alternative is to have the server hold on to the entrée orders and punch them in when he or she sees fit, based on how quickly the guests are eating their appetizers and based on how long the server thinks it will take to prepare the food. But in reality, there are too many variables for even the most talented server to be able to forecast accurately how long a lamb will take, how many monkfish we can pick up at once. Only we know precisely what is going on in the kitchen at any given moment, and thus only we know precisely how long certain things will take to prepare in that moment. So it's essential that we have all the information for all the tables as soon as it becomes available, and in the most consolidated form possible — one ticket.

Even when multiple-course tickets are punched in appropriately as one unit, they are not necessarily without difficulties. Special instructions can be a nightmare. There is only so much that can be entered in the POS system's ticket template. For meats that require a choice of doneness, there are buttons built in that say *rare, medium rare,* etcetera. For pastas that are available in vegetarian format, there are buttons that say *no meat.* These basic instructions are called "modifications." But outside the basic modifications exists a whole world of consumer possibilities, which, quite simply, would be impossible to accommodate with buttons on the computer. And so the server must type in these special requests by hand: *light on the garlic,* or *no salt or pepper, add extra olive oil on the side.* But since servers are often in a rush, and space is always limited, and there's seldom a rigid formatting standard, what you end up seeing is something more like this:

```
1000023589              FRI 12/7/12
CANDICE                 TBL: 36
18:17                   GUESTS: 2


************************2************************

*************************************************

              HOLD FIRE

*************************************************
1 SKATE
  L.O. GLRIC
  seat 3

1 PORK LOIN
  M.W.
  NO SP SUB EXT OO SOS
  seat 4
```

The permutations of interpretation are almost limitless; the ticket becomes a Choose Your Own Adventure story. Sometimes you need clarification from the front of the house.

Back waiters like Hussein can often help. They overhear the servers' conversations with guests; they see orders being punched in. Plus, because they usually resent the servers — for being short with them, perhaps, or for making more money than they do — back waiters are always eager to jump at any opportunity to sort out the dimwitted mistakes of the waitstaff. But since they're not having those conversations with the guests, and since they're not punching in those tickets, they can't interpret everything. Which is why the server's name is always on the ticket as well.

Chef snaps in the direction of the back waiters. Hussein appears in an instant.

"What on earth does this mean?" Chef says.

"I don't know, Chef," Hussein says. "Fucking Candi, so stupid."

"Get her in here," Chef says.

And Candice will rush in, nervous, flustered, to explain the ticket.

The only logical system, especially once service begins to accelerate, is to send out tables in groups. These groups are called "pickups." As expediter, Chef choreographs the pickups. He does so by maintaining a steady line of communication with the front of the house and by keeping track of what food has gone out. As Catalina and the entremets chug out appetizers, Chef rearranges the corresponding tickets in their new order, the order in which second courses will be served, depending on what appetizers go out first. This is the way the flow is developed. Four or five tables get their first courses, and then the cooks start on the second courses for those tables, while Catalina proceeds with the first courses for the next batch.

Chef must also keep track of the productivity of all the stations, their comparative levels of busyness. If VinDog on meat entremet is bogged down by pastas, Chef will rearrange the next pickup so that it's meat-light. If Warren can't get to the pass on time with the fish garnish, Chef will rejigger the pickup to accommodate him. If Catalina is inundated with salads and desserts, we'll slow down all hot food until she catches up.

Once a pickup is set, there's no turning back from it. Chef calls out the tables by number, and the cooks say "*Oui,* Chef" and sequester the four or five dupes in the pickup section of their boards. Since meat and fish are most sensitive to time, Julio and Raffy have a brief conference when the pickup is called. They decide, based on their respective levels of readiness, how long it should take.

"How long?" Julio belts out.

"Four," yells Raffy.

"Four," confirm the rest of the cooks.

Every station has a digital timer. When

the time is decided, each cook sets his or hers, and away they go, stirring, sautéing, searing. Only cooking sounds can be heard at this point, pops and fizzles, bubbles and squeaks. This is when the din is so rhythmic it can be mistaken for silence. Everyone knows what he has to accomplish and how long it must take him to do so, so there is no need to talk about it. All withdraw into a place of internal focus, saying next to nothing until the timers chime.

"To the pass!" everybody says when they ring out. The pans come soaring in and the food gets plated. "Service!" Chef says when the plates are ready. The back waiters pick up the plates and take them out into the dining room.

This is where your work on the pass becomes more involved. In addition to tasting all the food, you also need to organize it. What seems like a simple four-table pickup might comprise a dozen pans on either side when it arrives at the pass. This is a lot. Chef can't be sorting through each pot and pan in search of the right food. You need to huddle them up by plate for him and even further segregate plates by table — these turnips are for table 7, while these are for table 25. This work is important because each pan of food has an identity and a destiny. It was marshaled onto the stove purposefully by its cook. Perhaps the John Dory that Raffy put down for table 19 is a bit big, and, seeing this, Warren adapted a particular pan of garnish to fit the fish properly. Perhaps VinDog sees Chef plating table 22 first and knows that of the two mafalde he's got ready, one was started earlier than the other and should thus go out first, with 22, since they've ordered one. Perhaps there's a PPX table — *personnes particulièrement extraordinaires,* the VIPs — and Julio knows that one rib-eye was marbled more handsomely than the others, a choicer cut. He'll tell you this as he passes it over to you and it's your responsibility to take note, make sure it gets where it needs to go.

You are the kitchen's middleman, the crucial catalyst in the chain reaction of service. There's an oral transaction that happens between you and the cook when he delivers items to pass. It's cooks' argot, which you must interpret and communicate to Chef as necessary.

"This cassoulet is the veg-head on 9," Warren says. *"Sin tocino."*

What he means is that, of all the pans he's giving you, this particular portion of beans has no bacon in it, satisfying the special request of a vegetarian guest seated at table

9. Overlooking such information could be devastating for the guest and for the restaurant, especially in cases when the special request derives from allergy. But Chef is not always available to have these sorts of conversations — he's busy plating and expediting, or fielding questions from the front of house managers, or arranging special canapés for preferred clientele. So you have the conversations, at close range and in quiet voices, to avoid interfering with the work of others.

These transactions are not limited to special requests and ticket modifications. There is a host of other information that you're there to provide the cooks with as well.

"Gimme an all-day on venison," Julio says. He wants to ensure that the tickets he has on his board mirror the tickets on board at the pass, and that he has enough meat working to cover everything that's on order. You inspect the tickets and count up the deer.

"Ten all day," you say. "Six on fire. Three MR, two medium, one M-dub."

"Good," he says, with a wink and a nod. "That's what I thought."

"Those herring ready yet?" Raffy groans, wondering if the fish for the special have been cleaned.

"Brie's on it," you say. "No sweat, nothing on board."

"*¿Tenemos más aceite de ajo cocinado ahi atrás, verdad, güero?*" Catalina asks.

"*Claro que sí, doña,*" you say. "There's always more garlic oil."

These interactions create a bond that is central to the flow of service. It's keeping tabs, checking up. Cooks need to know these things, but they might be timid about asking Chef such questions directly, for fear of trammeling his concentration or simply looking obtuse. While Chef is always tuned to every wavelength of the kitchen (he's a virtuosic eavesdropper), he's not necessarily paying attention to such moments. So the cooks confirm where service is at with you. You are their go-between. It is your responsibility to ensure that everyone is informed. You do so throughout the first seating by way of quiet conversation.

This is where synergy is important. Your performance here directly affects your future success. The second seating hovers over you like the sword of Damocles. And there is no lull between now and then. Service spools up steadily. You must stay ahead of the curve. Pickup after pickup must issue from the kitchen flawlessly. Taking extra time on one project is robbing time from the next. And the projects are adding up. There is no time for refires now. There is no time for errors or miscommunication. Everything must be crisp and clean, cooked perfectly, so that when a hundred eighty people descend upon the restaurant around eight o'clock, you come correct.

In cooks' parlance, the closest relative of the idiom "come correct" is *soigné.* Soigné (swän'yā) is taken in Standard English to mean elegantly done, well groomed, sleek. In the kitchen it means, essentially, perfect. First-quality ingredients prepared using the best possible techniques and served in the most beautiful fashion. Etymologically, it is the past participle of the French verb *soigner,* which means to care for or look after, the way a nurse would, or a loving mother.

You always want things to be soigné. Every table is PPX, every guest is a VIP. They all deserve to be looked after, cared for. We are here to cook for people. *Alimentation:* the provision of nourishment — this is what we do. And we continue doing it long into the night, not because we favor adversity, but because we know that in doing so we get the chance to create with our hands something that sustains people and brings them joy. And because we know that in all the details, all the minutiae, all the intricate flourishes, difficult and tedious as they often are, can be seen the sincerity of what we do. And even though our days are hard and congested and misaligned, we know that through persistent focus and discipline and effort and care, we have the continual opportunity to do something genuine.

There is plenty of time in the first seating to cook this way, with love, as they say. But as guests multiply, so do their orders. There are more tickets to decrypt; there is more food to be made. It gets harder and harder to find the time to do things right.

And now the dining room is beginning to get loud. You can hear the rumble from the kitchen. The second seating is arriving. It's eight o'clock — showtime. Your throat tightens. Printers begin to buzz.

"Hear that, boys?" Chef calls out. "Let's do this. Ordering: two herring, one agno, one tartare. Followed by: two fluke and a rib-eye, MR."

"*Oui,* Chef!"

"And . . ." he says, "picking up on 17, 9, 32, 47."

"*Oui,* Chef!"

"Four!" Julio says.

"Four!" comes the echo.

Timers are set, pans clank about, burners blow on, the sizzle sounds swell. Smells abound of melted fat, aromatics, and caramelization.

"Plates!" says Warren. You reach below the surface of the pass and produce a fresh stack of china. He heaves the plates off the table with a huff.

"Kiko, *sarténes*!" yells VinDog. Kiko slides a pile of sauté pans onto Vinny's flat-top. Neither has time to make eye contact.

The timers say we're two minutes out but the entremets begin lobbing up their pans in advance. There's no time to mess around on this pick, and they know it. There's not space on the table for every pan and every plate, so they start bringing them early, throwing them on flame-tamers and trivets where you can reach them.

You start tasting. The lentils are good. The carrot puree is adequately fluffy. The potato salad is impeccably dressed.

The endive, however is hammered. Where it's supposed to be a beautiful golden brown, it's black as coal. You send it back.

"Again," you say.

"*Oui,* Chef," Warren says. He activates a new pan on the flat-top, splurts oil into it, swishes it around.

You take a mouthful of risotto. It's under-done and short on seasoning. You slide the pan back onto the flat-top, splash it with chicken stock, dust it with salt. You sample the cassoulet. It needs acid. You dribble in some sherry vinegar. Warren wouldn't be able to fix these things quickly enough.

"Pull it together, Warren," you say, firmly but gently. "We haven't got time for this now. I expect more out of you."

"*Oui,* Chef," he says. Sweat beads on his forehead.

Meanwhile, Catalina is in the weeds on garde manger. With the influx of new tables, she's buried in appetizers. You dash over to bail her out.

"Yo no necesito ayuda, pendejo," she says. *"Necesito estos platos que se quita de la ventana. ¡No tengo espacio, puto!"*

"*No hay pedo,* baby," you say, and you begin to remove the plates from the window above her station. As you do so, she begins to load a fresh set in. "Service!" you yell.

Hussein hustles over. "What table?" he says.

You look at Catalina. *"Veintidós,"* she says.

"22," you say. "Apps on 22. And come right back here for the next round when you're done." You hand the plates off and dash back to the pass.

169

Timers ring out.

"To the pass!"

Everything is coming up now. It's impossible for Chef to plate this whole pickup alone. You and Stefan jump in. Stefan takes to dumping pastas into bowls, you take to smearing swatches of carrot puree, laying down lentils. Your presentations aren't as fetching as Chef's, but they're in the neighborhood. It is the best you can do.

"Service!" Chef yells. A parade of back waiters stalks in. They pluck up the plates two by two and usher them out to the waiting guests.

"Next pick: 13, 22, 11."

"Oui, Chef!"

Pans hammer down again. More splutters, more sizzles.

Four minutes evaporate.

Timers go off. Food sails to the pass. Back waiters grab it up.

The sound of the printers is ever present now. The space between orders has shrunk to nothing. Not even a second. When one order stops printing, the next starts — impatiently, as though it's been waiting. Your focus, out of necessity, switches from doing things perfectly to simply getting them done. All you can do now is try to make them as good as possible. Chef's focus, out of necessity, switches from plating most of the food to plating nearly nothing. All he's got time for now is expediting, making sense of this river of tickets.

"Order fire!" he belts out. "One monk, one goose. Shit. Julio, how long on those birds?"

Julio has just recently put a fresh tray of geese in the combi, but they're still way out.

"At least ten, Chef," Julio says. "Plus they have to rest."

"Call it twenty, then?"

"*Oui,* Chef. I'm sorry, Chef."

Chef studies the ticket. "No, no, hold on," he says, preoccupied by something on the dupe. He flips through the dead tickets on the spike until he finds what he's looking for. "Son of a bitch!" he says. "I knew it! Hussein!"

Hussein materializes in a flash from behind the kitchen's swinging doors. "Yes, Chef!"

"Get Devon in here, now!"

Devon, the usually shrewd star server, has made the fatal mistake of taking expediting into her own hands. She punched in a table's appetizers, then waited until she saw fit to send in their entrées on a separate dupe. Of all things, goose and monkfish require the most advance notice; they take the most time to cook. She should know this.

After a minute, she slinks in. Chef gets right to the point.

"How many times do I have to tell you to punch the whole ticket in all at once? How fucking hard is it?"

"But, Chef, it's a deuce. They're a couple on a date," Devon says. "They were taking so long to decide, I thought —"

"When I want your opinion I'll ask for it. In the meantime leave the expediting to the professionals."

"But —"

"These people are going to wait twenty minutes now," he says, crumpling the ticket and chucking it at her. "Because you like to do what you please."

She desperately petitions Julio's help in speeding up the order.

"Julio," she says. *"Puede —"*

"Listen, *mami chula,* an error on your part does not constitute an emergency on mine," he says. *"No soy mago, bebé."*

"Look, Devon," Chef says, raising his voice. "If you want to keep your job, you'll shut your mouth and get the fuck out of my kitchen."

Stefan steals a sympathetic look at her. She stares back at him despondently, as if to say *Help me out here.* But there's nothing he can do.

"Sorry, Chef," she says.

"Out!" Chef screams.

The cooks go silent.

You have a look around.

Everyone is shaken, yet thankful that Chef's anger foamed over on her and not us.

Everyone except for Stefan, that is. His face has gone rosy pink.

We all wait for the call.

"All right," Chef says. "Where were we? Right, let's finish this pick on tables 22 and 23, plus bar: 9, and then move on to the twelve-top at table 37."

The cooks slide up their food for the two tables and the bar customer and immediately start work on the big table.

"How long on big table?" asks Julio.

Just then, there's a commotion on the fish side.

"Aw, fuck *you,* guy!" yells Warren.

A pan of garnish hits the floor. Its contents splatter everywhere.

"*¡Hijo de la chingada!*" shrieks Catalina from garde manger.

"What is it?" asks Stefan, leaning over to see what the fuss is about.

It's Raffy. Apparently he was wrong — he

173

can't handle it. He's not going to make it. He's doubled over, bracing himself against his station's lowboy refrigerator.

A gag can be heard. A hot splash.

He's vomiting into the trash bin beside his station.

Everything stops.

The only sounds are Raffy's ralphs and the printer spewing tickets.

The moment seems to last forever.

"Saw this one coming a mile away, huh?" Chef says.

The gags turn to dry heaves. Raffy's got nothing left in him anymore. He is broken.

"Sure did," you say.

"Well," Chef says, clapping you on the back. "RTG?"

"*Oui,* Chef," you say. "Ready to go."

You need to solve this problem. You run to the office and grab your gear: Peltex, offset, forceps, spoons. You grip a cake tester in your teeth, shoulder a set of side-towels.

Kiko is sloshing up the vomit when you return.

"*Puto borracho,*" he mutters, dipping past you with the grotty mop.

The station is a disaster area. Mise en place everywhere. Fish strewn all about, some cooked, totally hammered, already garbage, past the point of no return; others raw but for some reason seasoned to death, drying out, becoming useless; still others (the herring for the special, to be precise) in various stages of being cleaned, their viscera spilled out over the cutting board. *What on earth was this kid doing?* Most of this fish, it seems, can't even be accounted for. At least, it's not on order — the station's ticket rack is empty. Yet, ahhh . . . Here an avalanche of tickets clings, untouched, to the printer. Pathetic. He didn't even have it in him to keep his board organized. And now the whole kitchen is five minutes behind because of him.

You look back to the pass. Chef's attention is all on you. His brow is twisted in a mixture of anger and confidence. He gives you a nod. You nod back.

"*Oui,* Chef," you say.

Now it's time to cook.

Cooking is an exercise in kinetic awareness, economy of movement, mastery of the senses. You can smell when a sauce is scorched; you can hear when a fish is ready to come off the plancha. You must trust these senses to help you through the night. Your whole body must remain active. No matter what recipes you know, no matter

175

how much experience you have, each piece of fish in each pan presents a unique set of circumstances to which you must react, based on the sensory information at hand in the moment. You must take what you have before you and make something lovely out of it. And while it might be the same thing every day, it's something new every second.

Since there is rarely only one guest ordering food in the dining room, it is rarely possible to do only one thing at a time. While one hand waggles a saucepan of demi-glace, the other lights the burner beneath a *sautoir,* to make it hot for the next piece of fish due to go down. While one hand lays that piece of fish on a drop tray to be seasoned, the other reaches for the salt. If you spin away from the stove to toss a piece of trash into the bin, you take the opportunity to grab a fresh side-towel from your station before spinning back. When your hands are full of mise en place you've just pulled from the fridge, a soft hip check brings the fridge door home. To take a pan from the stove, open the oven door, place the pan in the oven, and close the oven door is one fluid motion. While you read through the tickets on board, you keep busy cutting, chopping, stirring, sniffing, listening — all with a sense of urgency.

To watch a good cook work well on his station is to witness multitasking of the highest order. But not all cooking happens within the wingspan radius of a cook's personal station. It is not a one-man show, it is a collaborative effort. There is stretching, bending, leaning, and opening. There are infiltrations, encroachments, interferences. There is path crossing. There are truncated alerts — "Behind, hot," "Door open," "Knife" — which help everyone know what is going on around him so that collisions can be avoided.

While no environment is free of accident and human error, the ability to work collision-free is expected of any good cook. In good restaurants, everyone works this way, with *sprezzatura:* a certain nonchalance that makes their actions appear to be without effort and almost without thought, an easy facility in accomplishing arduous tasks that conceals the conscious exertion that went into them. They instinctively move about one another in the narrowest corners without even the subtlest brushing of hips. There are no burns or cuts, no pans dropped, no spills or messes made. Its practitioners call this performance "the dance." And while its choreography comes naturally to those of a certain acumen, it is important to develop proficiency in it if you have any hope for advancement.

In our kitchen it's not a lack of experience, intelligence, or skill that compromises the dance; it's that rare occasion when one of the cooks lets his emotions best him. He's hungover, his mind is elsewhere, he suffers from a temporary bout of indolence, forgetfulness, unpreparedness, disorganization, anger. In this state he can't see clearly the deficiency of his own work, and it isn't until an especially time-sensitive moment that he realizes the error of his ways with a grumble — "Oh, shit!" — and must spin or dash, and thus spills and splashes, burns himself, and messes up the station. And the messier the station gets, the harder it is to maintain organization. And the less organized you are, the more frequent the "Oh, shit!" moments. It is cumulative disruption.

Right now, Raffy has really screwed the pooch. Apart from fish lying everywhere and tickets getting backed up on the printer, his work this evening has been untidy, to put it mildly — detritus abounds. An hour's worth of splatters encrusts the stove's piano; the oven's handle is slick with smears of grease; the spoon water hasn't been changed since the beginning of service; the cutting board is filmed with fish tissue.

It would be impossible for you to work the remainder of the night with the station in this condition. You'd constantly be re-adjusting your technique to accommodate the mess. Your instincts tell you to put things that need cutting down on the cutting board, but since you know that fish guts have been rotting on it all night, you can't do that in good conscience. You'd have to stop, think for a second, and find an alternate surface. You'd be losing precious seconds every time you did this, and you'd spend the whole night a step or two behind. The only way you'll be able to catch up is by taking a moment to wipe everything down, refresh the spoon water, and change out your board.

"Yo, Juan," you say, "this spoon water looks like the East River, dog. Do me a favor and change it out for me, will you?"

Warren drops what he's doing and jumps in to help you get organized.

"This sack of shit better pull it together," he says, dumping the spoon water into the sink and filling the bain up anew, "or I'm out." A rare moment of recalcitrance from him.

"I think he's done for the night," you say, loading in a new cutting board. "You're not going anywhere."

"I don't understand what Chef sees in him," he says with a shake of the head. "Anyways, so who's gonna cover the station?"

"Me," you say, shuffling your tools into place.

"Oh," he says. "Sorry, Chef."

Just then Marcus, the front of house manager and part owner, swings into the kitchen cradling an armful of plates. He's got refires.

"These flounders," he announces, presenting Chef with a pair of fish, "they're *rare.*"

His Brooklyn accent is thick and insulting. His eyes are dark with moral turpitude. He plonks the plates down on the pass before Chef irreverently, throws you a nasty glare, and storms back out into the dining room. Chef studies the plates a moment. Vasculature materializes on his forehead; his earlobes go purple as if gearing up to steam.

He lifts the plates in your general direction.

"Fix it," he says.

He grips the plates firmly as you reach to take them from him. You look up at him. Your eyes meet. The look on his face seems to say *Never mind what Marcus says, he's a total piece of shit. I know you didn't cook this fish. I know Raffy is to blame. But now we need to fix it.* It's a relatively comforting look. Some glint in his eye even seems to say *We are in this together. It's you and me now.*

"Oh, and by the way," Marcus says, poking his head back through the kitchen door, "the *Times* is here. At table 6."

The refires were the last fish that went out before Raffy went down. They looked beautiful then, but the customers have cut them open to reveal a gash of raw flesh. It tears you up to see fish like this. You should have known they were underdone when they came to the pass. You should have been able to tell. You should have taken a cake tester to them. They shouldn't have gone out. It's embarrassing. But at this point, it's no use lamenting the situation; you just need to fix the problem. And you realize now that you need to do it before the order for table 6 arrives. You had almost forgotten that the *Times* was coming in.

When magazine and newspaper writers arrive, all the focus switches to them. Even if they aren't proper "food critics" — if they write for the business section, say, or they have a travel column — the work they do is still public and the things they say can reach

181

a large audience. That's not to say that all public figures receive this attention. Hollywood personalities, for example, despite how they may be treated by the front of house staff, rarely arouse any special effort from the folks in the kitchen. Nor do political celebrities or sports stars. But people who write for periodicals always strongly affect cooks because they have the unique power to advance a chef's career — or obliterate it, depending on what they say. So the instant the name of a publication drops, ears perk up and the mood shifts. You still give plenty of attention to all the other tables, but your focus transfers from ensuring the magnificence of *their* dining experience to giving yourself ample time to satisfy the writer.

But first you have to rip through these refires and clear the board as best you can. You pull down a stack of pans and scatter them about the flat-top. Oil goes into two. You take two cuts of fluke from the fridge and place them on a clean drop tray. You pat their flesh dry with a C-fold towel and season them with salt, pepper, and freshly cracked coriander seed. When you season, you season from a height so that the spices sprinkle down like a light snowfall, evenly coating the surface of the fish. The pans you use are heavy-bottomed steel sautoirs, with a copper inlay, so they're hot in no time. You lay each fish, one by one, into its own dedicated pan. You swirl them around to ensure that they don't stick before letting the stove do its work.

"Up in three on the refire," you say to Warren.

"*Oui,*" he says, readying the accoutrements.

"How long on the twelve-top on 37?" Julio says, with something of a grin on his face. He likes it when you have to work on the station, and he gets a kick out of being ahead of you.

"Six," you say, confidently. "And 42, 15, and 9 in eight, *oui*?"

"*Oui,* Chef," everybody says.

Monkfish, skate wing, arctic char hit the pans; herring, wreckfish, and gambas hit the plancha. You flip and sizzle, slide pans side to side, slip some into and out of the oven, shove others into and out of the salamander. In three minutes you're ready to head to plate.

"Let's do it," you say, and you make your way to the pass, where Chef and Stefan are in the fray laying waste — slicing meats and stabbing tickets something fierce. The sweat beading on their foreheads matches yours.

"Stef," you say, "let's get new plates on

that refire."

"Oui," he says, thrusting up the china.

You're almost caught up when the printers begin to buzz again. They've been quiet for a while, which is curious since you know the dining room is full. The quietness suggests that the waiters have been busy elsewhere and haven't had time to punch in tickets. All their focus has been on cosseting the *Times* table up front. This buzzing we hear now is probably the order. It is a big one, and when it's finally done printing, all the cooks cock their heads toward Chef to listen as he plucks it from the pass's printer.

"Ordering," he says, pausing to look over the dupe in its entirety. "PPX. Four-top." He glances up at you with a raised eyebrow. "Two herring, one gambas, one green-lip, one tartare. Followed by a monk, a fluke, a mackerel, two char, and a cheeks."

This order is frustrating. Not only are there six entrées on order for a table of four people, but they're almost exclusively fish. And the first courses, with the exception of the tartare that Catalina picks up, are all hot appetizers to be made by you as well. You look up quizzically at Chef; he shrugs as if to say *Sorry.*

"VinDog," he says, "after apps go on 6, be ready to pick up four tastings of the veal tongue pasta."

"*Oui,* Chef. Four soign-dog agnos, heard."

"And, Catalina, let's put out a round of canapés to start."

"*Sí, Jefe. ¿Cuáles?*"

"Do Kumamoto and uni first, then the foie-lychee drops," he says.

"*Sí. ¿Cuántas?*"

"Four and four."

It's the best Chef can do to help. He'll send out these complimentary dishes because they're blindingly easy to prepare and the minutes it takes the *Times* table to eat them will buy you an extra moment or two to pull together their real food. In some sense he's sticking his neck out by doing it. Letting food critics know that they are being pampered is terribly gauche — it throws a chef's confidence into question. But given the order that's come in, it's basically unavoidable. You need the time to collect the VIP set.

In good restaurants, all the ingredients are choice, sourced from the best farms and purveyors, harvested at their peak, sustainable, free of chemicals, and so forth. But when a PPX table sits down, you sift through your mise en place to find the choicest of the choice.

The green-lips should all still be tightly

shut. Mussels open when they die, exposing their interior meat to the elements and accelerating the spoilage process. In order to be sure you have the freshest ones, you dump a couple dozen into a deep Cambro of cold water and wait to see that they float, which indicates that they are airtight, still alive. They should also, while they're in the cold water, be thoroughly cleaned and rid of their beards. Their shells should be brown like almond skin at the base and blush into an electric viridian at the rim. They should be huge, but also similar in size, so that they pop open at approximately the same time when you steam them. The prawns for the gambas dish should also be uniform in size and shape, but other features help you decide which to sell as well. They should be plump and hold their shape firmly. Their shells, legs, and digestive tracts should be cleanly removed, showing no sign of the butcher's touch in doing so, and their heads and tails should be soundly attached, so that they don't fall off with the administration of heat. Still other features help you pick out the herring. Their eyes should be clear and there should be no sign of decay on the fins. Their skin should be a brilliant aluminum tone and should wrap neatly and fully around a stout belly. If the eyes are cloudy or the fins are frayed, the fish is old. If the skin has begun to change color or peel away, the fish is old. And if the fish is old, you don't use it — not for the *Times*.

The canapés have been sent out by the time you've selected the right food, and since they're only *amusebouches* — small bites, mouth pleasers — they won't take long to eat. So you don't waste time waiting for the server to fire the apps.

First are the gambas, because they take the longest. You lay them on the hottest part of the plancha so that they can Maillardize without overcooking in the center. Then come the green-lips. You pour them into a screaming hot copper pan, hit them with a knob of butter, drop in four fingerfuls of shaved fennel, a spoonful of garlic confit, a splash of wine, and a dollop of soubise, then cover them with an inverted *sauteuse* and let it ride. You flip the gambas and drop the herring on the plancha.

The green-lips are ready when they've all gaped their maws. The orange meat is supple and glimmering. The liquor from the mussels has bubbled together with the butter and wine and soubise to form a viscous emulsion that coats the whole pan. They're finished with a few drops of lemon juice and a flutter of fines herbes; a quick toss in the pan and into the bowl. The gambas come off when their spotted heads go coral red and a caramel-colored sear veils the opalescent white of the flesh. They land in a terracotta cazuela on a pillow of black romesco, and finish with a dusting of pimentón dulce, a sprinkle of bottarga di tonno, a stalk of compressed scallion, a parsley pluche. The herring come off as soon as their aluminum flesh goes umber. You pop them on a drop tray, pass them to Chef for plating. And just like that, you're out with the apps.

Even though VinDog is sending out a middle course of pastas, you still need to begin work on the entrées immediately after sending out the appetizers. First is the monkfish, which you select based on size and symmetry. You want the biggest piece you can find, and you want it to be rolled into the tightest, most perfectly cylindrical roulade possible. Also, you want to be sure that the transglutaminase is fully set, so that the fish doesn't open up on you when it hits the pan and starts to seize. You dust it with Wondra flour and slip it in.

The chars and mackerel go down next. You pick them based on their relative proximity to the head of the fish. You don't make friends with tail cuts; they are too thin and cook up poorly. You want a thick piece from the head end.

All three have skin on them, which means they need special attention in two specific ways. First, before they're cooked, their skin must be dabbed completely dry with paper toweling. This encourages the development of crispiness, which in turn optimizes chewability and deliciousness. Second, once they begin cooking, they must be held down. When fish skin hits hot oil it immediately seizes up, which causes the entire cut to buckle, forming an arch over the cooking surface. As a result, the edges that remain in contact with the cooking surface develop a beautiful sear, while the part in the center that is raised is undercooked and simply steams. So when each cut of fish with skin on it hits the pan or the plancha, you firmly but gently press it flat against the cooking surface and hold it until the subcutaneous collagen hydrolyzes into gelatin, elasticizing the bond between skin and meat and allowing the cut to remain flat and cook evenly. This, of course, takes only a matter of seconds, but it's an essential step.

Finally the fluke. You take the largest, most evenly cut piece you have, the squarest pavé, from the youngest, most athletic fish in the fridge. After a liberal seasoning, you lay it down.

Three minutes later, all the fish are nearly done. You bring them to their final internal temperature with a few repetitions of arrosé. Julio only has veal cheeks on the pick, which he's been able to prepare at his leisure, since this order is your show. All that's left now is to wait for confirmation from the front of the house that the mid-course pastas have been cleared. While you wait, you shepherd each pan about the cooler areas of the flat-top to avoid over-cooking. Once Chef gives you the go-ahead, you bring the food to the pass and go to plate.

The skinned fish are crispy to the tap; the fluke wears an amber coat; the monk shaft is sheathed evenly in a caraway crust. All the cuts are plump and dripping with juices. They are perfect. Soigné. A spritz of essential oil from the zest of a lemon finishes them off.

You cut the monk open. You are not quite satisfied. You give it a few seconds under the salamander. The foie goes molten. Now it's ready. You slide it to Chef with a flare of pride. He nods without needing to look up. He takes it to plate with the expected measure of gusto. Hussein and the back waiters file over and scoop everything up.

"Take it down, baby," Chef says, clapping

Hussein on the back.

And out goes the food for the PPX table.

As expected, indulging the *Times* has set us back on the food for the rest of the guests. A blitzkrieg of tickets has piled up, two dozen tables — at least. This is where the hammer comes down.

"Fun don't stop, boys," Chef says. He reads off another ticket. Or maybe he calls out the next pickup. The distinction between the two is becoming hard to identify. It's difficult to pay attention now.

"*Oui,* Chef," we say to his calls. The vim wanes. We're all so inundated with information at this point that it's challenging enough to keep track of what we are doing presently, never mind what we are supposed to be preparing to do in the next five minutes, the next fifteen minutes, the next hour. No movement is distinctly its own except in the sense that it comes before or after another in a constant chain of busyness. The pickups blur together. Everything becomes one motion, for just this very moment. We switch to autopilot.

Finish one fish, move to the next. Start with a hot pan, start with hot oil. If it's not hot, wait. Don't start early; it'll stick. Check the oven instead. There's something in there. It needs to be flipped. Out it comes. In goes the butter. Let it bubble. Crush the garlic. *Arrosez.* Flip. Arrosez again. Put a new pan down. Season the bass. Always from a height. The bass goes in. A monk looks done. Give it the cake tester. It's barely warm. Another minute. To the pass with it. Three chars go down. Their skins soufflé. Press them to the heat. Hear the crackle. A pan is too hot. The oil smells scorched. Start again. Burner at full tilt. Now for the mussels. They jump in the oil. Aromas flourish. Here is a branzino. First of the night. Score its skin. Into the Griswold. Its eyeball pops. Flip it over. Into the oven. On with more gambas. On with more pans. On with more burners. Scrape down the plancha. Wipe down the piano. Towel your brow. Printers buzz. A new pick. Six more fish. Your legs are tired. Tickets blur. Chef needs more. "Next up . . ." Cooks moan. "*Oui,* Chef." Fat splutters. Timers chime. Food goes. Tickets are stabbed. New ones are plucked up. Organize the board. Start again. Eight fish now. A pan to each. Eight butters. Eight garlics. Eight flips. Eight arrosés. Eight plates . . . eight more picks. Machine-gun frequency. Clean pans from Kiko. They're getting heavy. They drop on the flattop like a bullet blast. Your arms are stiff. The branzino is done. Swing open the oven. The heat blazes. It dries your eyes. Blink it out. Grab up the Griswold. Bring home the door. The towel is wet. The pan burns your hand. Dizziness. Nausea. Synesthesia. Pain. This is normal. This is what we do. We are in this together. We are almost there.

An hour vanishes before you snap back into consciousness and realize that all this time you've been operating entirely on instinct. The thought is jarring. You emerge disoriented, knees buckling like a newborn foal's. It's a moment before you can figure out what has brought you back to life. And then it hits you: You've just sent out the last piece of fish you had cooking. There are some tickets on board, but nothing is fired yet. There is nothing working. You are finally caught up.

The station is messy. You take this opportunity to do a clean sweep of it. You look around the kitchen. Everybody is red-faced and sweaty. But they, too, are tidying their stations. They're folding their towels, changing their spoon water, surveying their mise en place. They slug seltzer from quart containers, belch, and stretch. They have made it through the push. And so have you.

Just then you remember that you have half a cigarette that you clipped earlier on before service started. You extract the soggy packet from your pocket. The cardboard is frayed, the cigarettes bent out of shape. You pluck up the clip with a fishy pair of fingernails.

"Off line," you say, and make your way past Warren toward the loading dock. Chef winks at you as you pass him. You smile and raise an eyebrow. Out back you kick the door open and light up your smoke.

MESSAGE

The kitchen is quiet when you come back. Like a battlefield after the defeated have made their retreat. There are still plenty of customers in the dining room — we don't officially close for another hour — but the night's vise grip has slackened significantly. Hussein stands at the pass examining a handful of tickets that have arrived in your absence. You have a gander — mostly desserts.

"You good, Don Juan?" you say.

"Claro," Warren says, tossing a neatly folded towel onto his station's spick-and-span tabletop. "We got nothing," he says, running a hand suavely through his blond locks.

"Good," you say. "Start that slow breakdown."

You find Chef in the office, changing into street clothes. His droopy boxer shorts and scrunched-up tube socks humanize him.

"Nice job today," he says, slipping into a pair of loose-fitting fleece pants. "You really picked up the slack for your boy."

"Thanks, Chef," you say. "Why does everybody keep calling him my boy? I hate that kid."

"Yeah," Chef says, pulling on his overcoat. "Tell me about it."

"And he's getting worse every day," you say. "I don't know what his deal is, but he really needs to pull it together."

"Well, I mean, he knows his shit. He's a good cook. And when he's not rip-shit hungover . . ."

"Yeah, but when is he ever not?" you say.

"Yeah," Chef says.

"I mean, seriously. And poor Warren? Get outta here. That guy works a hell of a lot harder, and faster, and *cleaner,* and he has to be cleaning up fuckface's messes every time he turns around. And Juan's like thirty-two. Could you imagine that? Working en-tremet for someone ten years younger than you? And, Chef, I gotta tell ya, I was on that station today after him — *ram*shackle, bro."

"Yeah," Chef says, biting at a hangnail, staring thoughtfully at the wall. He exhales deeply. "What do you think I should do?" he says, looking up at you. "Should I get someone new?"

"I mean, I think we gotta at least bring a couple people in to trail. Throw Raffy back on prep, scare some sense into him . . . What about Warren?"

"Not ready," he says, sputtering out a piece of cuticle.

"I don't know, Chef, he's —"

"Not yet, man," Chef says. "Trust me. Warren needs another six months in the pot. Do you really think he could handle fish? On a night like tonight? Hell, no."

"Yeah, you're probably right," you say. It crosses your mind to bring up the virtue of trial by fire, but it's usually best to just defer to Chef in these situations. He has been evaluating cooks much longer than you have, after all. But something in you wishes to disagree with him. "Raffy is just *such* a shithead, though," you say. "And frankly, I'm tired of having to jump in for him every time he decides to tie one on."

"Aww, poor baby," Chef says, pinching your cheek, giving you a light smack. "We're cooks, don't forget."

"Yeah, but —"

"Listen," Chef says. "I'll have a talk with him this week, after the weekend's through. In the meantime, let's get an ad out and see who's out there. Never know, maybe we'll get someone good."

"That's true," you say ruminatively. "I hadn't even considered that."

Suddenly the idea of finding someone new shifts from being a problem to being an exciting prospect. Your instinct is to go for homegrown talent, to cultivate from the ground up, rear cooks from *commis* through *chef de partie* and onward. But who knows what blue-chip fish cooks are out there looking for work?

"All right, anyways, whatever," he says. "We'll figure it out later. But now I need to get the hell out of here. What time is it? Shit, eleven-thirty? My wife's gonna kill me."

"Wife? Maria?"

"No, Julia."

"Oh, *ex*-wife."

"Technically we never got divorced."

"What happened to Maria? I liked her."

"She thought I was cheating on her."

"Who'd she think you were cheating on her with?"

"My wife," he says.

"And now you're meeting up with your ex-wife?"

"I only have one wife. Julia. It's the same person. Listen, it's a long story," he says. "Anyways, whatever, I'm out." He grabs up his bag and heads for the door. "You're on brunch tomorrow, yeah?"

"Yeah," you say.

"You're in early, then, right? What, eight, eight-thirty?"

"Sounds about right."

"All right, just keep an eye on the pass until Stef's done with inventory and then get the hell out of here."

"*Oui,* Chef," you say.

You love working the pass in Chef's stead, getting a taste of what it's like to drive the bus.

"Oh, and Hussein was saying something about there being dick for staff meal today?"

"Right, yeah —"

"Just make sure those guys get something. Herring, pasta, whatever. I don't give a shit. That's just the last thing I need to hear outta Marcus's stupid mouth, some shit about staff meal. I've had it up to here with that guy."

"*Oui,* Chef."

"Oh, and another thing," he says. "Rojas told me he found a pan in the garbage can out back today. Any idea what's up with that?"

"Oh, yeah," you say. He's talking about the pan you broke toasting the filberts. "The handle broke off."

"So you throw it out?"

"Yeah, I thought —"

"Your girlfriend gets sick, has to have her tits chopped off, you gonna throw her out, too?"

"No —"

"Come on, baby," he says. "If you ever wanna make the big bucks, you gotta start using your head for something other than a hat rack."

"*Oui,* Chef," you say. "Sorry."

"All right, *papi,*" he says. "Whatever. Don't worry about it. Have a good rest of the night. And, again," he says, slapping you five, "nice job on the line today."

"Thanks, Chef," you say.

"Later," he says.

And out he goes.

With Chef gone and service rounding to a close, you have a minute to take a breather in the office and ready yourself mentally for the morning. Brunch is always a catastrophe, usually right out of the box and always right to the bitter end. Tourists show up early; leftover party-goers stay late. And they all want their food fast, so you turn tables quickly. You'll do another three hundred covers — at least. But whereas Friday night dinner service is a seven-hour meal period, the three hundred you'll do for brunch tomorrow will be crammed into a five-hour slot, ten to three. So it is important to be well prepared, well in advance, to keep the ball from rolling away.

Rogelio and Brianne get a head start on brunch mise en place on Fridays. They do the bulk of the heavy lifting, usually saving only the à la minute work — hollandaise, circulator eggs, etcetera — for you in the morning. When it's busy, though, as it has been today, they tend to accomplish less of this work, because they get caught up in resupplying the line. You've instructed them to leave a note for you on such occasions, so you know what you'll be walking into in the morning. You grab up your clipboard and see what it says:

Cheff,
Las papas de los hasbrowns están cortados en la nevera. Los huevos están rotos. El tocino están en los sheet trays.

Vamos a terminar todo en la mañana junto. Te amamos, putito.
XOXOX Rojas y Bri

So they've managed to crack the eggs, dice the potatoes, and sheet up the bacon. There is still plenty to do, of course — the sliced mojama, the pulled duck confit, the coriander puree, the herb yogurt — but it could be worse. They have gotten *some* things done. Some of the bigger projects, actually. Anyway, both of them are due in for doubles tomorrow at 0600, so they'll have four hours before service starts to put together the rest.

That should be plenty of time, you think.

You notice an arrow drawn in the bottom right corner. You flip the page to find another message, this one from someone else altogether. It's a hyperrealistic pencil drawing of a penis, complete with a hairy pair of testicles. From the head of the penis springs a dialogue bubble in which are inscribed, in very neat, almost architectural script, the words Sac up and get some drinks with me tonight dickface. This note is not signed, but it's got Stefan's name written all over it.

It's ten till midnight now.

You begin to realize how little sleep you'll be getting.

So much for getting out at ten o'clock, you think. *So much for meeting up with Vera. She's gonna be so pissed.* You pull out your phone and type her up a message:

HEY BABE. CRAZINESS TONIGHT. HAD TO WORK THE LINE. RAFFY WENT

You hope it's not all gone to smash. After the way today has gone, you could sure use a drink with Vera.

You're waiting for her response when Hussein pokes his head into the office.

"Chef," he says, "we need you on the line."

"Come on, Hussein," you say. "You can expedite, can't you? I've been here since nine in the morning, man."

"No, Chef," he says. "It's Chef Juan. He need your help with the fish."

"Ugh . . . Orders?"

"Yes, Chef. Many orders."

"Son of a bitch," you say.

Out on the line, Warren is getting rolled. A battery of tickets has piled up on the fish side since you've been gone. He's doing his best to get it all done, but he is struggling. He is utterly flummoxed. All the garnish is set and he's attempting to prepare the protein to go with it, but he's having trouble volleying both at once. He can't do it alone. He's clumsily arroséing a skate wing when you arrive. The butter has gone black in the pan, and the skate is without sear, a pale white save for the scorched butter solids collecting in its crenellations. Some wrecked accoutrements lie cold and moistureless on a drop tray; an emulsified sauce boils at full tilt on the flat-top, shattering into a million pieces. It's a real hatchet job here.

"How you doing, bud?" you say, clapping him on the shoulder. "You okay?"

"*Oui,* Chef," he says. "Just workin' a couple orders."

His ears have gone a vibrant red. There is a deluge of sweat pooling on his crumpled brow, dripping into his eyes. He blinks it out with his long blond lashes, fixes his eyes on his work. He is trying very hard and failing. Chef was right — he's not ready.

"*¡Oye, sous jefe! Limpiarlo?*" Julio says, bumptiously. "*¿Que pasó Juanita, todo bien? Quiero limpiar!* You no ready, baby?"

"Fuck you, Julio, you fucking mutt!" Warren says.

"Yeah, chill, Julio," you say, throwing over a glare. "Not the time."

"Okay, Chef," Hussein says. "I need it table 14. They wait very long."

"For fuck's sake, Hussein, give us a second," you say. "What's with you people? We're not fucking *pulpos*!" You smack a fresh set of pans down on the flat-top. "Come on, Warren, let's do this shit," you say. "Me and you. Don't listen to these

204

guys, it's just me and you here."

"*Oui,* Chef," he says. "Thanks."

It sounds like tears in his voice.

Just then, as you're reaching into the low-boy for a fresh piece of skate, your phone buzzes in your pocket. You take a quick look. It's a message from Vera:

IN BED BABE. EXHAUSTED. CAN'T DO IT. MAYBE TOMORROW. XO

God damn it, you think.

Stefan materializes at the pass. "Everything all right out here?" he says.

"Livin' the dream," you say.

"You get the message?" he says.

"What message?" you say.

"What do you mean, what message?"

"What do you mean, what do I mean? What fucking message, guy?"

"The one on your clipboard," he says, with a full-faced grin.

"Oh. That. Yeah," you say, humorlessly.

"So?" he says. "Drinks?"

You look back down at the message from Vera. You look at Warren's incinerated skate wing smoldering on the stove. *What a mess,* you think.

"Yeah," you say. "We better get some drinks."

Close

Of the many aphorisms emanating from the kitchen, one of the sounder ones is the notion that you are only as good as your final plate. It doesn't matter how well you've performed throughout the evening if you can't offer the same level of care and execution to the last diner that you did to the first. Judging by the dishes you're assembling now, you feel comfortable believing that you are good at what you do. Your fish is cooked perfectly, your plating is debonair. This meal is soigné, as are the people waiting to consume it.

"Service!" you yell, and Hussein and the back waiters scuttle over to retrieve the plates. As the food walks, you unfasten the top button of your coat. "Start breaking down," you say to the cooks.

"*Oui,* Chef," they say.

"LOI, Chef?" Warren asks.

"Not sure yet," you say. "You know the

rig. Don't throw anything out. I'll go have a look now."

You trudge through the kitchen doors and into the dining room to determine whether the last order is in.

Out front the atmosphere is alien. Lamp-light and candles offer a sharp contrast to the kitchen's fluorescent wash, and it takes your eyes a minute to adjust. When your vision has come to, you take in the scene.

Guests are sparse. The few that remain are mostly two-tops, couples scattered here and there engaged in intimate colloquy and canoodling. A stray quartet of burly, steak-eating men huddles around a distant table, merrily guffawing over tall glasses of dark beer. A small gaggle of pert college girls giggle and gossip with Marcus at the far corner of the bar. The mood is generally pleasant, and over the murmur of quiet conversation can be heard the tinkle of jazz. On each face is a look of serenity. Everyone is happy. It might bring you joy to think that these guests are happy because of something you've provided them, but sheer exhaustion prevents your thoughts from wending that way.

You spot Hussein standing beside the service bar, surveying the dining room with great attention. In this environment he car-

ries himself with an aplomb that goes un-
noticed in the harsh light of the kitchen.
His posture is erect and respectable, his
countenance cool and collected. He is digni-
fied out here despite his rank.

"Talk to me, *papi,*" you whisper. "LOI?"

"No, no," he whispers back, waving a
finger. "I think one more order." He directs
your attention to the group of underage gig-
glers at the end of the bar.

"It's ten past one, homeboy," you say.

"Friends of Mr. Marcus," he says.

"Asshole," you say. "He and his wife just
had a kid, right?"

"Yes, Chef."

Just then, Marcus notices you down the
bar. He gives you a nod and excuses himself
from his conversation with the girls. He
makes his way over to you with long ar-
rogant strides, his gait marked by intoxica-
tion's signature self-awareness.

"Hey, man, I got one more order coming
in," he says. "We're taking it right now, then
that's it."

It's happening: that last table on a busy
night that manages to squeeze in an order
after closing time. There's frustration in the
moment, of course — everyone is battered
and wants nothing more than to be done.
But nobody is surprised, because it happens

all the time. And there's some solace in it, too. It's good sometimes to know that there is only one more to go. To know that in ten or fifteen minutes it will all be over. Because you can do anything for ten or fifteen minutes.

"That's cool," you say. "Always ready. How did we do with the *Times*?"

"Yeah, yeah," he says. "They were fine, it was great. Just do me a favor and take care of these girls, arright? Make it nice, yeah?" His lips peel back in a wicked grin, revealing a mouthful of crooked teeth stained purple with wine. "How hot are these broads, bro?" he whispers, fisting you one in the arm.

You raise an eyebrow and have a look down at them.

"No problem, sir," you say, and make your way back to the kitchen.

You return to find that the cooks have begun the closing procedures. They've delivered all the smallwares — cutting boards, pots and pans, foaming guns, and so forth — to Kiko to be washed. They've kitted up their mise en place in plastic delis and Cambros, logged and labeled it, and tucked it away in their lowboys to be sorted out in the morning. They've doused all their stations' surfaces with soapy water and are going at them with green scrubbies and squeegees. All that's left after this is the postservice menu meeting.

And so the monkey business has commenced. Chef coats have been unbuttoned, hats and gloves have been doffed, and the boys have taken to cracking each other with wet side-towels and cackling wildly over adolescent jokes about dongs and butt-cheeks.

It's an important moment, this, our gallows humor. It boosts morale, serves up an extra portion of joy. What a sin it is to have to interrupt it with more work.

"One more table, guys," you say, setting off a chorus of groans. "They're putting it in now."

"Uh-uh, Chef," Julio says, defiantly. "I already turned my grill off."

"Well," you say, "turn it back on."

"We closed ten minutes ago," he says.

"I don't give a shit what time it is, you're not done until I say so."

"This is bullshit," he says.

But Julio knows he's in no position to argue with you. He throws down his scrubby in a huff and fires up the grill.

"That's more like it," you say.

Just then, you spot Hussein in the dish

area, picking through a bus tub of dirty plates in search of something salvageable to eat. It's a pitiful scene; heartbreaking to imagine him returning home to his wife and children, smelling of the kitchen, with nothing but scraps in his belly.

"Oh, and Julio," you say. "Now that the grill is back on, why don't you fire off a few hanger steaks?"

"Yeah, right," he says. "For who?"

"For the back waiters," you say.

"No way," he says. "I'm not here to cook for them. No ticket, no food."

"I'm not asking," you say. "Put 'em on the fucking grill."

Even though you've used his misfortune as an opportunity to turn the screw on Julio for his tactless behavior, Hussein still sees this as a Promethean gesture on your part.

"Thank you, Chef," he says earnestly.

"Take this, too," you say, lobbing him a pint-size deli of pommes purees. You give him a nod and make your way to the office.

Stefan is in there putting the finishing touches on his inventory grids.

"Bro, what the hell are you still doing here?" he says.

"No shit," you say, plopping down into your chair. "I'm about to break out. You done with inventory? Can you cover the line?"

"We closed ten minutes ago, guy."

"Yeah, but there's one more order being punched in now. Some bimbos Marcus brought in. Bar menu."

"*Pshhh.* Whatever," he says. "Here, have a cold one." He opens the minifridge, looses a can of pilsner, and lets it fly your way. You crack it open. The sound is therapeutic. You take a swig and let it linger. You throw your feet up on the desk and close your eyes.

"So, where to?" Stefan says, after a moment. You open one eye, train it on him. He cracks a can of beer for himself, flicks away the suds with a snap of the wrist. You inhale deeply and close your eyes again.

"I don't know, man," you say with an exhale.

"Don't be a dick, dude," he says. "You already said you were down for drinks. So where to? Fat Black? The Inveterate?"

"But we have beers here," you say.

"Bro," he says.

"Sure," you say, swallowing another guzzle. "The Inveterate. Fat Black will be a shit show tonight."

"All right, great," he says. "The Inveterate it is."

He stands up, tilts his head back, and

sends his beer home in a single blast. He crushes the can and pitches it into the bin. "Lemme go close this bitch up and then we can break out," he says, barreling toward the door, stopping only to belch before pushing his way back into the kitchen.

A relieved fatigue descends upon you when he leaves. The office is yours again now. Your asylum. Your refuge. What kitchen clangor can still be heard through the walls fades to nothing. No more burned hazelnuts. No more monkfish roulades. No more three hundred covers. It is all over. Tonight is through. You kick your shoes off onto the floor beside you. You fold your arms over your chest. You sink even farther into your chair.

The last order is always a paltry one: charcuterie, salad, mussels — low-hanging fruit of this sort, which the cooks are able to dispense with lickety-split. That most late-night diners are willing to receive the food "as it comes" makes the work even easier. Once Hussein scoops up the final plate, the gas feeds are cut, the heat lamps are shut, and the cooks launch the terminal cleandown. They pull up the black carpet runners and shake loose the crumbs that have collected throughout the night. They remove the slim-jims from their trash chutes, knot up the thick black bags, and deliver them to the dumpster out back of the loading dock. They set all the ovens on a cleaning cycle and set all the overnight projects on a slow roll. Then they sweep. Then they scrub the equipment. Then they mop the floors. Then they polish the stainless to a shine.

Within twenty minutes, the kitchen is vestal again, as though nothing ever happened. A few sponges and squeegees and sprays of the hose, and every vestige of activity is wiped away. If it weren't for the Z report, there would be no evidence to suggest we did twenty thousand dollars in sales today. Three hundred meals, along with everything it took to get there, exist now in memory alone.

After the clean-down, the cooks get changed. It's at this time that they begin discussing their prep lists for the next day. Tonight's business has decimated mise en place. Everyone's agenda for tomorrow is full to the gunwales. Julio anticipates several hours of meat fabrication, while Warren and VinDog brood over daunting amounts of sauce and vegetable work. Even Catalina, who usually sets herself up for days at a time, vents about what a tough day she has ahead of her. Some tasks can be delegated to Rogelio and Brianne, but the two of them already have plenty of their own work to do, so they can't pick up much. It's beginning to look like the whole team is going to be in the weeds. And the fact that brunch service will be happening at the same time only exacerbates things. Time and space and manpower will be in very short supply. So it is important to hash out a strategy tonight. Who has large projects that will consume ovens and stovetops? Who needs to get in and out of the dehydrators and circulators? What is going on the list for the A.M. crew, and what can people do to help one another out? These are the questions that get batted around while the cooks take turns slipping into and out of the cramped locker room.

It's this discussion that populates the menu meeting. When the cooks have figured out all their individual responsibilities, put together a rough list of tasks for the A.M. crew, and divvied up any overlap items (things that are used on multiple sections, such as onion soubise or crispy garlic, which could be done by prep cooks but always turn out better in abler hands), they present the information to Stefan. As closing sous chef, it is ultimately he who decides their fate. He is the one who knows what tomorrow's reservation books look like. He is the one who has some sense of what Chef might be fiddling with for tomorrow's menu. He is the one who, at the end of every day, hunches over paperwork, calculating pars and protein counts and product in-house, deciding what needs to be added to standing orders and what needs to be fetched from the market in the morning. So he is the one who finalizes the prep lists.

When all the cooks have finished changing clothes, everyone convenes at the pass and the meeting begins.

Suddenly the sound of printers buzzing jolts you to attention. *Order fire, six monkfish.* The dreadful thought hits you: *We're out of monkfish!* A rush of adrenaline. *I need to solve this problem.* You grope around in search of your gear. Your eyes dart about in a blur. *Where the hell are my shoes?* you wonder. *I'm so screwed,* you think.

It's a minute before you realize you are still in the office, still alone. No monkfish has been ordered. There is no problem that needs your solving. You've simply dozed off.

I need to get the hell out of here, you think.

With great effort you pull yourself upright and stand. The tile floor beneath you is cold and unyielding. Your calves have gone taut;

your feet have swelled up like sugar toads. You hobble over to the closet and peel off the chef's outfit.

Back out on the line, the menu meeting is in full swing. Warren and VinDog are engaged in a spirited debate over how much lime juice needs to be squeezed by the A.M. prep crew.

"I'm telling you, a quart is *way* too much," Warren argues. "I have half a deli in my low-boy alone, never mind the two-quart in the box."

"Yeah, but how long has that shit been in there?" Vinny retorts. "I like my acids to be bright and delicious, dog, don't you get it? I'm not about to use your shit. It's mad old. It's a fucking chemistry experiment by now."

They notice you coming out of the office in street clothes. The conversation stops.

"Listen, fellas," you say. "I hate to interrupt your lovers' quarrel, but I gotta bounce."

"Word," Vinny says, extending a hand for the slap-up. "The Inveterate?"

"You going?"

"*Hell* yes."

"Warren?"

"Ehhh . . ."

"You're such a bitch, Juan," Vinny says.

"Bro, I dry-heaved in a garbage can on Sixth Avenue this morning. Is that not good enough for you?"

"A wise man once told me, 'If you don't gag every morning, you're not living life to the fullest.' "

". . . he said, unzipping his pants," Warren adds.

"Bro, I will shove my —"

"All right, guys. Enough," you say. "You should come, Warren. Celebrate a good night of work. Nothing too crazy. I'm here early tomorrow, so I won't be out too long myself."

"Doubt it!" Vinny teases.

"All right, I *may* be equal to the task," Warren says, reluctantly.

"Whatever," you say. "Think about it."

You start slapping everybody goodbye fives. Stefan grips your hand extra tight when you get to him, gives you a surly look.

"Don't disappoint me, man," he says. "None of this Irish goodbye shit of yours. You better be there when I get there in twenty minutes."

"All right, mac. Relax," you say. "I'll be there. Doña Cata — *cuídense*. Kiko — *está chingón*, baby. *Nos vemos mañana. Gracias a todos.*"

"*Sí, jefe, gracias,*" they say. "*Nos vemos*

mañana." It doesn't even cross your mind to invite any of them out, because you know what the answer would be — *gracias, pero no gracias.*

"And as for the rest of you," you say, "I suppose I'll see you when I see you." You give a wink to Stefan, to throw his faith in you into question. He tosses back an evil eye.

"You better be there," he says, with a point of the finger.

You snicker mischievously. "I'm out!" you say, with a salute.

In the shadows of the back corridor you pop the hood on your toggle coat, thrust open the heavy metal door, and leave the kitchen.

BAR

Outside, the world has been transformed. The sun took any trace of warmth with it many hours ago when it set, and now a frigid breeze twists the leafless trees up and down the street. The only sounds you hear are the crinkle of ice beneath taxicab tires, the distant twitter of bibulous partygoers, the muffled rumble of express trains passing under you.

You are standing at the foot of the loading dock when your ears pop — first one, then the other — and the pressure that the kitchen's heat had been trapping in your head is finally released. As a result, the quietude becomes more expansive. The hushed thrum of silence gathers around you. The sensation is both satisfying and sinister. On one hand it makes you feel alive, free of the cage, at one with the outside world; on the other hand it makes you feel unsafe and alone and very far from home. You light up a cigarette. The wind picks up a bit. Something like a shudder stirs somewhere inside you. You exhale a billow of smoke and set off toward Sixth Avenue, where there are sure to be more streetlights and at least a few more people.

Against your better judgment, you decide to keep your word and go to the bar, if only to bid your colleagues a proper adieu immediately upon their arrival. Thankfully, everyone has agreed to eschew the neighborhood's harder-rocking establishments in favor of the Inveterate — an industry mainstay. It's the sort of place where fist-pounding footballers are scarce and forlorn hipsters are even scarcer; where there's enough room around the pool table to play a comfortable game, and you don't need to scream at the top of your lungs in order to be heard by the person beside you; where articulate barkeeps deal draft beers off the arm, and florid-faced locals nod their heads to tunes off the blues-suffused jukebox.

In the wintertime, the front windows of the bar are perpetually obscured by a mantle of condensation, which lends a pleasant softness to the hearthlike luminescence but makes it difficult to tell what's going on inside. Only silhouettes can be made out from where you stand on the curb finishing your cigarette. By the looks of it, though, some of your favorite regulars are in there holding the fort. And past the brass draft taps and stacked bev naps, on the opposite side of the bar, can be seen the towering form of Peter O'Malley, the six-foot-six salt-and-pepper barman, who dishes out jumbo whiskeys in between fielding people's problems.

Excellent, you think. Pete is your favorite bartender.

He spotted you on your way in, and he's already getting your drinks together by the time you find a stool.

"Petey-Pete," you say, extending a hand. "What's up, guy?"

"Hello, old friend," he says, his deep voice betraying the faintest lilt of brogue. "How was your night?"

"Madness," you say. "Like three hundred."

"Oh, dear," he says, skating a pilsner and a whiskey rocks your way.

"Thank you, sir," you say, dropping a twenty on the bar.

"That had to be brutal," he says.

"It was no walk in the park, I'll tell you that much."

He pours himself a whiskey to match yours.

"Well," he says, raising the glass. "In the words of my father, *'Is crua a cheannaíonn an droim an bolg.'* " He bangs his glass into yours and throws the liquor into his gullet.

"Right," you say, taking a sip. "What the fuck does that mean?"

"Aghh." He winces. "The back must slave to feed the belly." He winks at you and, noticing some needy customers down the bar, heads away. "Think about it," he says.

The whiskey wants to come back up at first. You are incredibly dehydrated and your throat quivers when the astringent liquid hits it. A crisp light beer, though, is the perfect antidote — a refreshing splash of effervescence that lubricates the palate and the tongue. After a few seesaws between the two, you start getting a glow on and you begin to believe that the stiff liquor tastes like some toothsome honey and that the beer is merely fizzy water.

Your head starts to swim.

Your mind wanders back to the restaurant. Even though you've been released from its bondage, it's difficult for you to ever really leave. You sip your whiskey and picture what is happening in your absence.

Having covered closing before, you can easily imagine what Stefan is doing right now. This is *his* Zen moment in the kitchen. It is *his* temple now, *his* domain. Everyone else has left; he alone remains. He stands at the pass, arms folded, looking over the place like a king in the making. Where there was once a wild excitement, there is now a placid stillness. He reassesses the evening's events in his head. He notes our moments of strength, reckons up our missteps, considers how we can do better tomorrow.

You signal Pete for another round.

He's pouring your whiskey when you notice someone at the far end of the bar whose stooped figure your eyes come to rest on with attention. He is teetering on his stool, bent over himself as though he's just had his ribs kicked in, feebly grasping at an empty glass. You squint in an effort to make him out. And then it hits you — it's Raffy, of all people. And he's razed to bits on beers and whiskeys again. *This fucking kid,* you think.

You grab up your drinks and storm over, ready to haul him over the coals.

It's just in the nick of time that you've gotten Raffy out of the bar and into a cab. Stefan would have flipped out if he knew Raffy was here getting sluiced after his epic washout on the line. Who knows what sort of clash would have come to pass. But as it went, after a few craven attempts at levity on Raffy's part, you were able to yank him outside, jam a few bills into his unsteady hand, and stuff him into a taxi before anyone else showed up. And now, just as his cab careens out onto Sixth Avenue, Stefan, Warren, and VinDog appear across the way.

Cooks always look different in street clothes. Without their chef whites, they shed that mechanical anonymity known so well to strict kitchens, and their real personalities come into focus. A ridiculous fur-rimmed parka accents Stefan's survivor's edge; a stately Crombie coat and scarf underline Warren's decorum; shredded dungarees and a studded leather biker jacket make Vin-Dog's irreverence all the more obvious.

If you didn't know better, you'd wonder what on earth this motley trio was doing fraternizing. But these appearances don't deceive you. You see the linkage here. Even if you didn't work with them you'd be able to tell. It's a certain way of carrying oneself that secretly helps any cook recognize one of his own. An outward air of strength and mental toughness, tempered by some undeniable tinge of anxiety. It's this juxtaposition of conflicting characteristics — which can be sensed in something as simple as a flash of the eyes or the flick of a cigarette — that helps us pick each other out, regardless of how we're dressed.

"What up," Stefan says as they join you on the sidewalk outside the bar. "I can't believe you're still here. I thought you were a goner for sure."

"I told you I would be," you say.

"Right," he says.

"No Dev tonight?" you say.

"No, she'll be here," he says. "Her and a couple others'll be right behind us. They had mad tips to sort out tonight, so they got held back."

"Good," you say. "I was worried Chef might have put her off earlier."

"Nah, she's all good. I talked to her after service," he says. "She knows the rig."

"Ah," you say.

"It's cold as balls out here," he says. "Let's get some fucking drinks." He throws open the Inveterate's thick wooden door and gestures for you to enter. "Age before beauty," he says with a flourish.

"And pearls before swine," you say.

By day we are craftsmen of military efficiency, by night we are scoundrels who need no greater excuse than a busy night of service to justify going headlong into the clutches of vice. And this particular Friday night — like all those that came before it, and all those that lie ahead — is no exception to that rule.

Stefan doesn't waste any time. His first move when he gets to the bar is to line up a bevy of shots with a row of beer chasers on back.

"Ehhh, not me," you say. "I'm good."

"Shut it down," he says, foisting the whiskey on you.

"Yeah, you're starting to sound like Don Juan over here," Vinny says.

"Eat a dick, Vinny," Warren says.

"All right, fellas, get 'em up," Stefan says, raising his glass. "To a great service, and an even better one tomorrow."

"To the mind's blind eye and the heart's ease," you add.

"Ah, Albee," Warren says. "I approve."

"What's Albee?" Vinny asks.

"It's from a book, asswipe," Warren says. "You'd have to be able to read in order to know anything about it."

"A cookbook?"

"No," you say, sympathetically. "It's a quote from a play by Edward —"

"Ah, who gives a shit," Stefan says, slamming the glasses together in the center. "Just drink, you idiots!"

Every kitchen has its Lothario, and VinDog is ours. His rough edges have furnished him with an animal magnetism that no one has been able to explain. But it works somehow, and he's all too aware of it. Immediately after the shots, he takes off reconnoitering for girls. After a lap or two around the bar, and more than a few good-looking options, he zeroes in on someone right in his wheelhouse: a well-upholstered woman done up end to end in tattoos and loud makeup. She sits alone on a couch out back of the bar, tapping at a cell phone uninterestedly, a pair of black fishnets crossed tightly before her, struggling to contain their fleshy cargo.

"Hello," Vinny says, with sugary inflection. "My name is Matt."

"Hi, Matt," the woman says. "What do you do?"

"I am a chef," he says.

"Oh, how cool," she says.

She uncrosses her legs and invites him to sit down.

It's not long before Devon shows up with a retinue of FOH staffers from the restaurant, including Rupert the new kid and Candice the true professional. They, too, look different in their street clothes. Elegantly dressed, well groomed, and sleek, you'd never guess that they just got off work. They look more like nine-to-fivers set to paint the town red than like restaurant people. But their pockets, freshly wadded with small bills, tell the real story. They made out well tonight and they are ready to throw down for some drinks.

But Stefan, being generous in an outmoded and financially perilous sort of way, won't allow any of them even to think about buying their own drinks. He flags down Pete and orders a round for the whole group. Somewhere in the commotion, a fresh whiskey makes its way into your hands. When everyone has been served, another toast is proposed to a great night of service, and all tilt their heads back and let the booze in. Capsized glasses hit the bar with a ripple. Stefan grabs Devon by a belt loop and pulls her in.

"What's up, sugar lips?" he says, laying a juicy one on her mouth.

"*You* know," she says. "Same shit."

She proceeds to peck him about the face with kisses.

"Aghh, Christ," Warren says. "Pull it

together, guys. We're in public."

"Y'all wanna shoot some pool?" Stefan offers.

"You know it," Devon says, and she and he and the rest of the FOH crew head over to the table.

Only you and Warren remain. Two seats have opened up at the bar and you commandeer them with a pair of geriatric groans. You sip your drinks and have a look around.

The place has gotten noticeably fuller in the last half hour. Dozens of new customers have arrived, almost simultaneously. You could have predicted this. All the restaurants in the area close about this time, and their crews, like-minded as they are, had the same thought you did: the Inveterate. It comes as no surprise. It's the place to go on Fridays. Everyone in the industry knows this.

And now here they all sit, waving twenties and fifties, waiting for beers and whiskeys, while the bartenders scamper around shaking drinks and popping bottles, doing their best to accommodate the push.

Pete, the veteran among them, shows no fear. Like a stud line cook in the throes of service, he's hit his rhythm, selling drink after drink with stone-faced sprezzatura.

He's flaming orange zests on a batch of old-fashioneds when he notices you and Warren down the bar. You give him a nod; he nods back. No matter how many people need a beer, he'll always take care of you first — you've been coming here for years. He hands off the drinks he's just made and makes his way past the gauntlet of bill-brandishing guests to where you sit.

"Gentlemen," he says, flipping down a covey of coasters. "What'll it be?"

"I'll have another pair when you get a chance," Warren says, jiggling an empty bottle.

"Sure thing, friend," he says. "And you?"

"I'm good for now," you say. "Early morning tomorrow."

"Right," he says, producing a bottle of the booze you drink. He tops off the glass in your hand, slips the bottle back into its special slot in the well.

"Thanks," you say.

He gives you a wink and, with a point of the finger, moves on to the next guest.

Warren is a good person to chew the fat with. He's a philosophical type — always ready for scintillating discourse. Having spent time in another line of work, he knows what the world looks like outside the restaurant industry. Unlike the majority of your colleagues, with Warren you can actually talk about something other than cooking. At least, you *could,* if you wanted to. Not that you ever do on nights like tonight. No, after a busy service, the discussion at the bar almost always orbits work.

"So," you say. "How do you feel?"

"How do I *feel*?"

"Yeah, about service tonight."

"I feel like I just got donkey-punched is how I feel," he says. "I got fucking rolled tonight."

"Yeah, I think we all got rolled tonight," you say.

"Not like me," he says. "I got my ass handed to me at the end there."

You have to exonerate him. He shouldn't be blaming himself. In fact, if you're honest, it's only because you left him alone on the line that he got into trouble with that last little push. Otherwise he did a great job handling tonight's unprecedented numbers.

"Quit beating yourself up," you say. "You did a great job tonight."

"Right," he says. "I'm just glad Chef wasn't still around to see me go down in flames."

"Ah, don't worry about him," you say.

"I just want to do right by him, you know?

I want him to believe in me."

"He does believe in you," you say. "You just need a little more time in the pot is all."

"Yeah," he says. He swigs his whiskey, shakes the rocks around inside, stares through the golden liquid to the bottom of the glass. "It's like, 'How do you get to Carnegie Hall,' right?"

"Exactly," you say. "You'll get there. Don't worry."

"Yeah," he says, and swigs his drink.

At this moment you recognize in Warren a certain quality that exists in you. It's a desire to impress, a hunger for validation, a need to succeed. You want to preserve this in him, protect it from hurt. You must shepherd him the way your mentors have shepherded you.

"So what made you switch into cooking?" you say. "Why did you leave entomology?"

"Why do I cook?" he says. "That's an easy one. There's no politics in the kitchen. No bullshit."

"I think you'll find that there's plenty of politics in the kitchen," you say. "Plenty of hoops to jump through."

"Yeah, but there's a big difference between jumping through hoops and being given something you don't deserve. Which is the sort of bullshit you don't see in kitchens. I mean, you don't become sous chef at a great restaurant without earning the position, right? You've been here, what, two years?"

"Yeah."

"And you were cooking for how many years before that?"

"Ten."

"So you should know this better than anybody: you have to *earn* it. And you earn it with the skills you develop through years of hard work. And those skills are what define you. Cooking is the last true meritocracy. All that matters is how well you can do the job. And with what level of finesse."

"Sure," you say. "I just think it's dangerous to believe that hard work is everything, that all that matters is 'earning' it. That kind of thinking makes it easy to forget what we came here to do in the first place."

"I know hard work isn't everything," he says. "But it does count for a lot. I mean, it validates everything we do. It makes it sincere, keeps us honest."

"Right," you say. "But I think you're missing my point. Let me put it to you this way: What are we here for? As cooks, I mean, what are we here to do?"

"We're here to feed people," he says. "To take care of them."

234

"Exactly," you say. "But don't you feel like sometimes we lose sight of that? Like, when we get all caught up trying to 'earn' it, we forget that we are simply here to feed people? And if we forget that, then what is all this hard work for? To impress Chef? To satisfy ourselves? And if that's the case, isn't professional cooking just another form of enlightened self-interest?"

"No, see, this is where you've got it wrong, friend," he says. "The self isn't even part of the equation. Cooking is altruism. It's not about you. It never will be. It's only about what you do for others. And *that's* what hits me where I live. There is honor in it."

"I couldn't agree more," you say. "Which is precisely why it doesn't matter what Chef —"

"What the fuck are you chumps talking about?" Stefan interjects, boisterously lunging into the bar for another round of drinks.

"Cooking," you say with a touch of irritation. "What's it to you, boy?"

"You're not pollutin' our cooks with this philosophy mumbo jumbo again, are you?" he says, with an elbow to the ribs.

"No, Chef," you say. "Just talking about cooking. Why we do the things we do."

"He pollutin' you, Don Juan?"

"Nah, nah," Warren says. "We're just talking shop. It's all good."

"Good," Stefan says, signaling Pete with a nod. "I hate when you get all brainy and shit. It just confuses everybody."

"Right," you say.

Meanwhile, VinDog has escorted his new friend to the jukebox. She seems to have taken a real shine to him. She stands close by his side, running her long press-on fingernails through his knotty Mohawk while he picks songs. His selections, mostly seventies and eighties tunes, strut that tenuous line between proto-punk and synth-ballad, a juxtaposition that has summoned more than one curious glance in the direction of the jukebox, Warren's included.

"Get a load of this chick VinDog's putting the moves on," he observes. "What is he thinking?"

"I haven't the foggiest," you say, sipping your whiskey. "Different strokes for different folks, I guess. Anyways, back to what we were just talking about. I think that's exactly the point. That's what counts for most."

"Wait, that's *what* point?" he says. "I'm confused. What were we talking about again?"

"Right," you say. "What I was trying to say is this: quit worrying about what Chef thinks. I mean, sure, you want to do things the way he wants them. It's his restaurant, after all, his name on the menu. And sure, you want to be able to believe you're not totally fucking shit up all the time, so a high five from the boss every now and again is nice. But at the end of the day, none of that really matters. At the end of the day, what matters is the guest. That person on the other side of the kitchen door. The one you'll never meet, the one who has no idea what you look like or what your name is. The one who trusts you to keep her safe, the one who is about to ingest what you have made. The one you are nourishing, taking care of, looking after — she is what matters. Chefs come and go, and restaurants and coworkers, too. Your time at any given place, with any given crew, is fleeting. But that guest? She will always be there. She is the constant. The one you are cooking for. And all the hard work — the focus, the discipline, the effort, the care, the techniques you practice, the recipes you perfect — it's all for her. And the second you forget that, the second you start cooking for Chef's praise or critics' accolades, for pride in yourself or for high fives from somebody else, that's when all the virtue attached to the work we do — all this honesty and

sincerity and honor you're talking about —
that's when all that shit goes right out the
window."

The idea seems to fly by without leaving
an impression on Warren. His gaze has me-
andered from you to Vinny and his new
friend, and now to Candice the true professional's voluptuous rear end, which he's
taken to scoping out without a shred of
civility. His inattention is aggravating. You
were just beginning to feel you were onto
something, and now his head is elsewhere.
It makes you feel like you're talking to
yourself, which makes you wonder whether
you're saying what you're saying for his
edification or for your own.

"Who knew how good Candice looked in
a skirt?" he says.

And, like that, the conversation is gone.

"Anyways, whatever," you say. "Food for
thought."

You sip your whiskey. You look at your
watch.

Suddenly you feel like just going home.

"It's getting pretty late," you say. "Almost
three bells. Should probably think about
calling it a night."

"Yeah," Warren says, eyes fixed, mouth
agape. "I think I'm gonna soldier on here

awhile, though. Burn a bit of that midnight oil."

"So much for dry-heaving in garbage cans, huh?"

"Yeah, well, maybe there's some truth in what Vinny said about living life to the fullest. And right now, Candice's ass is looking pretty full."

"Right," you say. "I'm gonna go burn one."

Out front of the bar you find Stefan smoking a cigarette with great focus, a slight sway in his stance. It appears the drinks have begun to catch up with him. *Great,* you think. You were hoping to make a clean getaway.

"What up," you say.

"You're not leaving, are you?" he says.

"No, no," you assure him. "Just having a cigarette."

"Good," he says, lighting your smoke. "Good night tonight, right? *Crazy* night!"

"Yeah, maybe a little too crazy."

"You can never complain about being busy, right?" he says. "It's the best problem in the world."

"Yeah," you say. "But I just hate getting pounded on the line like that."

"This is what we signed up for," he says.

"I suppose so," you say.

"Don't worry," he says. "Tomorrow will be better. That retard Raffy will sleep it off and come back strong."

"I don't know," you say. "I'm starting to lose faith in that kid."

"Really?" he says. "I think he's pretty good."

He has no idea that Raffy was just here getting twisted, that tomorrow he'll probably be the same as today. You resist the temptation to mention it — you don't want to kill Stef's buzz.

"Yeah, well, I'm not so sure," you say. "And the way things are shaping up tonight . . ." You pause to gesture at the rest of the team carousing inside. "I think tomorrow's gonna be kind of a shit show."

"Aww," he says, pinching your cheek. "You scared, Chef?"

"I'm never scared, Chef, it's just —"

"It's just cooking, baby," he says. "This is what we do: we work hard, we play hard. We break to *build.* And we always bring some soigné shit the next day, no matter what. Am I right?"

He raises his hand enthusiastically for a five.

"Right," you say, halfheartedly slapping him up. "I suppose so."

"Fuck, yeah," he says.

For the next few moments, all that's exchanged between you is the occasional cloud of cigarette smoke.

"So, listen," he finally says. "Lemme borrow sixty bucks."

"Are you shittin' me?"

"I'll pay you back tomorrow when I cash my check. You know I'm good for it. Dev's still a little pissed at me for not sticking up for her when Chef flew off the handle tonight. I'm trying to take her mind off it with some Korean barbecue."

"Right now? Where, K-town?"

"Yeah, that place Danja is twenty-four."

"Can't you just give her a massage or something?"

"Nah, dude, I'm not getting out of the doghouse unless I put some bibimbap in her face."

You let go an exaggerated sigh.

"Come on, man. Please?"

He looks at you like a dog with a biscuit on his nose.

"Ugh . . . All right," you say, pulling your last three twenties from your pocket. "But —"

"Ha-ha! Good looks," he says, snatching the bills. "I owe you big . . . Now let's go get some more drinks. This one's on me."

He winks at you and fake-punches you in the gut.

"Right," you say, slapping his hand away. "Lemme just finish this smoke. I'll meet you inside."

"All right," he says. "I'll go fire up another round."

He rifles his butt far off into the street and heads back into the bar.

It appears the drinks have begun to catch up with you as well. You find you need to spread your legs out shoulder-width across the sidewalk in order to keep a steady posture. Your vision blurs. You blink it out and study the scene back inside the bar.

Through the steamed-up glass you see Vinny and his new friend. You see them hand in hand, making their way toward the jakes. They stop at the restroom's threshold to kiss a minute, then enter together, presumably to either blow coke or have sex. Perhaps both. You see Warren putting the moves on Candice, whispering game into her ear. She fixes her eyes on him with great attention. He is obviously telling her something she finds fascinating. Perhaps he's teaching her about bugs. At any rate, you see she's gone sweet on him. You see Stefan, too, corralling a fresh set of drinks.

Presently Devon rejoins him at the bar. He takes her in and kisses her with profound affection. You see the spark of love between them, whatever that means for them.

You see most of these people almost every day. You spend most of your waking hours with them. More than with your family. More than with your friends. More than with your girlfriend. And you know more about them than you do about most people — where they are from, what they like to eat and drink, what music they listen to, what sorts of books they are into. You know what they like to do on weekends, what turns them on and off. You know their family histories, their religious perspectives, their relationship statuses, and their sexual preferences. You know their idiosyncrasies. You know their ambitions, their goals in life. You know what they look like when they are happy and when they are sad. You know what they look like when they are angry and frustrated and embarrassed and sorry and scared. You even know what most of them look like when they are in their underwear.

And yet somehow they feel quite unfamiliar to you right now — like estranged friends from some other period in your life. It's as if your connection with them is only a matter of circumstance, of time and place.

As if, were you working at a different restaurant in a different city, it would be a completely different set of people with whom you were so intimate. As if, were you to part ways with this restaurant and start at another, you'd also be parting ways with this group of people, leaving them behind in exchange for some whole new set of confidants whom you'd soon enough know everything about, too. And a nagging suspicion, which you'd prefer to ignore, wishes to assure you that not only is all this probably true, but also that this parting of ways might be much closer than you'd like to believe. That it always is.

None of these people are mine, you think.

A vague desolation begins to hollow itself out inside you.

You think of Vera. Her absence doesn't help. You look at her message again:

IN BED BABE. EXHAUSTED. CAN'T DO IT. MAYBE TOMORROW. XO

Maybe tomorrow?

Reading it over and over again only extends the perimeter of your loneliness.

Just then an abrupt change of music can be heard inside. Vinny's picks have concluded and Pete has taken over. First on his list is "This Charming Man" by the Smiths.

Suddenly you are transported five years into the past, to a restaurant you used to work at in Brooklyn. It was your first sous chef gig. Right up the block from the restaurant was a bar called d'Accueil, which the crew used to frequent after service. It seemed like every time you went there, "This Charming Man" was always the first thing you heard.

And then it dawns on you: *All* these people are yours. All the Chefs. All the Stefs, all the Julios and Raffys and Warrens and Vin-Dogs. All the Catalinas and Rogelios and Bries and Kikos. All the Husseins and Devons and Candices and Ruperts and Petes. Even sometimes all the Marcuses. These are *all* your people. Restaurant people. No matter what the circumstances, they will always be there. Whatever neighborhood in whatever city, state, country, or continent you find yourself in, you will always have friends nearby. You will always have people who get you. People who speak the same language, enjoy the same customs. People who work with the same sense of urgency, the same motivation. People who share your desire to feed, to nourish, to dish out the tasty bits of life. This is the bond you have with those around you. And it never goes away.

A smile tugs at your face.

All at once, the Inveterate's big wooden door starts calling you back.

You reach out a hand.

No, you think, putting yourself in check. *I better just go home before I get myself in trouble.*

You chuck the butt into the gutter and steal off into the night, full up with everything you need.

HOME

Out on Sixth Avenue, away from temptation, you take a few steps into the street
and throw your arm up in the air. It's late,
so traffic is sparse and taxis are hard to
come by. To make matters worse, it's nearing the shift changeover. Many of the cabs
that do pass by have already triggered their
off-duty lights. Those that haven't are either
already packed full of tipsy fare-splits or are
unwilling to make the trip to the outer
boroughs. Every now and then a Yellow Cab
or car service pulls over. "Where you
headed?" they say. "Brooklyn," you say.
Then they either say "Sorry" and zoom off
or they throw out some exorbitant figure
that no one on planet Earth would be willing to fork over for a three-mile ride. Either
way, you aren't getting any closer to home
like this. So after about fifteen minutes, you
resign yourself to catching a subway train.
You find the nearest glowing staircase and

climb down into the city's guts.

At the turnstile, a stiff bar to the groin apprises you of the fact that your unlimited ride MetroCard has run out of juice. You'd like to buy a new one, but the hundred bucks it'll cost you is not the kind of dough you're prepared to shell out at the moment. And you don't have any cash on you for a single ride. The last of your scratch went to Stef.

You have a look around: ghost town.

If anybody is in here, they're nowhere to be found.

Fuck it, you think, and jump the stile.

Only the night-shifters such as yourself ride the subway at this hour. An exiguous population of dozers and snoozers who seek cheap passage to the outer boroughs after work. They lean on pillars and pews patiently waiting, their blank gazes fixed on the dark tube in hopes that a pair of headlights will soon appear around a bend. When you reach the platform you find the first vacant column and join your kin, staring down the tracks with your fingers crossed for quickness.

The train is thinly populated when it arrives. You have your pick of where to sit. The best seats in the house are usually at the end, right by the adjoining doors. But tonight someone has spilled some suspicious substance there that suction-cups your sneakers to the linoleum. You take a seat in the middle instead, where you can use the long windows flanking the car like dim mirrors. After a moment's wait, the doors bong shut. The train chugs into action and crawls away from the station. As you enter the darkness, you inspect your fearsome reflection in the dusky glass across the way. It's the first time you've looked at your face since morning. It's not a pretty sight. The hours have fastened on you a mask of exhaustion. Pallid skin, dark luggage under the eyes — you look like you've spent the last two weeks in a black room examining microfiche.

I need a tan, you think.

You pop in your earbuds and lean back into your seat.

It was everything you could do to keep from falling asleep in the half hour it took to reach your stop. But now that you're back above ground, you decide you'd like to pick up a 40-ounce bottle of beer and sip it on the stoop for a while with some cigarettes.

Even though this decision defies all logic — you have to be back to work in five hours — it's an easy one to make. To wake up and go to work, come home and go to sleep, *iterum et iterum,* gets tedious quickly. In the interest of sanity, you need some downtime, some time alone to relax and unpack the day. When you never see the sun, you at least deserve some time with the moon.

You push through the jingling door of the twenty-four-hour bodega on the corner of your street. Oswald, a round-headed man of ambiguous extraction, is the clerk who works the overnight there. He has become something of a compadre to you over the years. You run into him almost every night. The morning guy, however, you couldn't pick out of a lineup.

"Oz, what's up, guy?" you say, placing your 40 on the counter.

"*You* know," he says. "Same shit."

"Camel Lights?" you say, pointing to the smokes behind the counter.

He passes you a pack and some matches. "That's it?" he says. "No sandwich? No ice cream?"

"Nah, not tonight," you say. "Hey, listen, I don't have any cash on me, I gotta use a credit card. Is that all right?"

"Ah, don't worry about it," he says, loading the bulbous bottle into a brown paper bag. "Pay me tomorrow."

"This is why I love you, Ozzie."

"Listen," he says. "One hand washes the other. I'm still waiting for you to bring me home some leftovers."

"I'll see what I can do," you say.

You grab the bottle by its fat neck and bounce.

Your stoop, steep and sturdy, is your place of repose — an after-hours sanctuary lifted a few feet off the sidewalk, where you can look over the peaceful, tree-lined street with the peculiar comfort that comes with being home at last. It is shaded from the glare of the streetlamps by the frozen growth of a tremendous elm tree, and because everyone else in this part of town is always asleep by the time you get home, it's very quiet and serene. Since the absence of light disturbs you less than the presence of noise, you find it quite a delightful perch indeed. You sit there most nights turning over the remains of the day, your soundless solitude disturbed only by the occasional mew of the feral cats that furtively comb the snow-laden neighborhood in search of nibbles.

You sit and turn your gaze to the hazy urban firmament. There is always a fuzz floating over this town. Even on the clearest evening, no more than a handful of stars can be seen. Few of them twinkle; none of them shoot. And still your eyes are drawn to them.

You think of Vera. Of being near her. Of twisting limbs with her. It upsets you that you didn't get to meet up with her tonight. You don't like the nights when you have to sleep apart. They make you sad. Especially when it is your fault for breaking the plans.

But is it really such a bad thing, to stretch out, get a good night's sleep, meet up with her the next day?

But tonight is not going to be a good night's sleep. And even if it were, you would gladly trade the best night's sleep to be with her. It is like a great weight being lifted off your shoulders when you slide into bed beside her.

But maybe this is a bit obsessive. Isn't it strange that you would need or want to see her *every* day?

But it makes you feel very good to smell her hair and hold her hand. And your time away from work is so minimal that you need to spend it as best you can: with her.

But what do you have to offer her in return? A few minutes before service starts? A kiss on the cheek before falling asleep?

You sip your 40.

You puff your cigarette.

You look up at the red moonbeams, wishing you could give her the half-light cloths of heaven.

When thoughts of Vera grow somber, as they often do at this hour, they recede to your mind's back burner with a shove from thoughts of work. It's almost impossible after a busy service to avoid going introspective, to avoid thinking back on what you did wrong and what you did right. The recollections come to you like snapshots strewn about a dining room table: now this moment, now that moment; now Raffy throwing up, now the *Times* showing up. And the collage they form gives you some basis upon which to evaluate the evening.

Was it a complete success?

Probably not. It did get hairy in there; vomit did happen. And who knows what the people at the *Times* table thought? You know you put out the best food you could, but once it leaves the kitchen it is out of your control. Diners sometimes see something totally different than what you send them.

Was it a total failure?

Again, no. We did take in three hundred guests, after all. The *Times* table *had* to notice how busy it was. And excluding the goose that got held up because of Devon's gaffe, and leaving off Raffy's blunder on his final flounders, everyone seemed to be well taken care of. We did put out some soigné shit tonight.

But it felt so very difficult at times. So relentless. So strenuous. How did Pete put it? The back must slave to feed the belly?

Perhaps there is some truth in that.

At the end of the day, you are a cook. A cook who wishes to be a chef. And if you have any hope of getting there, you can't let toxic thoughts like this take hold. You must be thick-skinned, hard as flint. You must pluck up courage. You must stay the course. *Service:* performance of work for another. *Alimentation:* provision of nourishment. *Soigné:* cared for, looked after, loved. This is what we are here for. This is what we do. This is the life we have chosen.

If you had the right amount of booze in you, you'd be content to stay up until that proximate dawn, swigging beers, smoking cigarettes, studying this soupçon of stars. For despite the chill, there is something warm about the stoop. It is as though this thick edifice, its brownstone balustrades cloaked in fresh pelts of snow, somehow insulates you from the bitter cold of the outside world. You could nestle here until the sun came back if you had to.

But eventually your defense mechanisms kick in. It's after five. You do need to get *some* sleep tonight.

Eight o'clock comes awfully quick, you think.

With a great heave, you hoist yourself up and begin climbing the steps.

When you arrive at your apartment, you fall immediately into bed.

You pull out your phone.

The screen is hard to read.

With arduous effort, you finger in the following for Vera:

GOODNIGYG SWRRTPEA

You hit SEND and surrender to sleep.

MORNING

The electric holler of your alarm jolts you to attention. A vague sense that it's been going off for a while now materializes in you, some faint recollection of weaving the noise into your final dream scenes.

You look at the clock on your bedside table. The digital glow is a blur:

08:27.

Oh, shit, you think.

You're due in in three minutes.

You spring from bed to find you're still fully clothed, toggle coat and all, in your outfit from last night. It crosses your mind to head out like this, to save time, to just go. But showing up to work in this clothing two days in a row won't do. Late or not, you need at least to change. Plus, you need at least to brush your teeth, to get this acrid taste out of your mouth, to get this fruity scent of booze off your breath. And you need at least to shower, if only a quick spin, to steam off the film of filth and vaporize the clutter of your mind.

The shower is unmemorable at best. Sleep deprivation and acute ethanol withdrawal have made a numb husk of your skin, and you can't even tell if the water sprinkling on it is hot or cold. Soaping yourself is confusing and slippery. You can't remember whether you've brushed your teeth. Yet, next thing you know, you're standing naked in your bedroom, trying to figure out what to put on.

But it's not until you find yourself in the backseat of a taxicab, hurtling at breakneck speed over the Manhattan Bridge, that you truly realize, with mathematical clarity, how horrible you actually feel. It's as if you've been body-slammed by a sambo specialist after running an ultramarathon. It's possible, given the ratio of hours of sleep to drinks consumed, that you are still a little drunk, which doesn't augur well. It means it's only going to get worse as the buzz wears off. The chances of today being better than yesterday are to hell and gone. It will only be with great effort that you make it through. And, judging by the way your throat threatens a gag every time you cough your deep morning cigarette cough, it's unlikely you'll be able to do so without throwing up at least once or twice.

But whatever, you think. *Let's do this.*

As the taxi touches down cityside, you're startled by the buzzing of your phone in your pocket. It's a message from Stefan:

NICE DISAPPEARING ACT LAST NIGHT GUY. I PROBLY SHOULDA DONE THE SAME. I FEEL LIKE A BEDPAN RIGHT NOW BRO. LOL. GOIN 2 B A FEW MIN LATE. HOPEFULLY I'LL GET THERE BEFORE CHEF. ON MY WAY NOW. HOLD IT DOWN.

Stefan typically comes in around 0930 for brunch on the weekends. When he arrives, you decide between the two of you who will work the line with Rogelio and who will hang out in the back prep area pulling together the mise en place for dinner. Since you get in first, you usually get to do whichever one you prefer. So it's a good thing he's also running behind today, other-wise he might have beaten you in and you'd be stuck cooking eggs all afternoon, which is never an attractive proposition.

You notice another message on your phone. This one, time-stamped at 0815, is from Rogelio:

¿DÓNDE ESTÁS CHEFF? TODAVÍA MU-
CHO TRABAJO POR HACER. CREO
QUE ESTAMOS EN LA MIERDA. ¿DEBE-
MOS LLAMAR JEFE VRYON?

You notice now that you've missed several
calls as well. They are all from Rogelio, too.
One after another after another. Every ten
minutes for the last hour, it seems. And
there is a gang of voice mails to go along
with them that all say the same thing: there
is still a lot of work to do.

This is bad, you think.

Of the whole crew, Rojas is least likely to
worry. He always keeps his composure. But
if this assault he's mounted on your phone
is any indication, it's safe to say he's losing
it now — big-time. Who knows what you'll
be walking into now? The falcon obviously
cannot hear the falconer. Will the center
hold? Will we be ready when the doors open
to customers? What rough beasts slouch our
way to dine today?

And, of course, since you haven't gotten
back to him, not even to let him know that
you received his messages, there is a good
chance that Rogelio has called up Chef in
hysterics. And if he has called Chef, there is
a good chance Chef will be coming in early.

In fact, there's even a chance he's already there.

This is really bad, you think.

Your throat tightens as the cab draws nigh unto the restaurant's back entrance.

The kitchen is the worst on Saturday morning. It's packed with people, and the impending brunch rush has everyone buzzing around flustered. Prep cooks rig up mise en place, back waiters kit up jams and jellies, servers roll up silverware sets. Crumbs have begun to collect on the floor; dishes have begun to collect in the sink. Every surface is covered with something. And the smells — of vinegared water and broken eggs and scorched fat — are ever present and overwhelming. And the noise — an incessant babel of pots and pans and plates and stainless — is only amplified by the droning flurry of the intake hoods. It's a veritable imbroglio. And service hasn't even started yet.

You round a corner to find that Chef has indeed arrived early. He stands stern at the pass folding a stack of side-towels. He has his back to you, but something in his posture says he knows you're here. Yet when you slip past him en route to the office, he merely leers at you out of the very corner of his eye, as if he barely wishes to acknowledge your presence. He looks livid.

Your limbs are stiff as you twist the chef's outfit around you once again. The cotton of the coat is cold on your skin; the wood of the clogs is inflexible on your feet. It's slow going today, and it's not going to get any easier.

It's nearing ten o'clock. The doors will be opening any minute now. Guests are probably already queuing up outside. You seize a Pedialyte from the minifridge, grab some gear — a knife, a spatula, a few spoons, a side-towel or two — and head into the thicket.

Before getting started, you must first interface with Rogelio. You find him in the back prep area slicing up day-old brioche for the *pain perdu.*

"Ay, Chef! I no see you coming!" he exclaims with an embarrassed grin. "I get scare and call Jefe Vryon," he says. "Sorry, no?"

"No, no," you say, extending your hand for the shake. "It's me that messed up. I'm the one who should be sorry."

"Ah, is okay, Chef," he says. "I think we gonna be okay now. We work together."

"Good," you say. "How we looking on the line?"

"Come," he says. "I show you. I think we ready."

Out on the line, it appears you actually *are* almost there. Despite your absence, Rogelio has succeeded in getting nearly everything together. He's even managed to arrange it exactly as you would. All that remains to be done is the brown butter hollandaise, for which the ingredients have already been assembled. You slap a sauteuse down on the flat-top and get ready to make the sauce.

Just then, your section's printer begins to make noise, as though your presence on the line were the cause. A ticket begins to emerge. You look to the pass. The printer there begins to activate as well. That mechanical buzzing sound fills the kitchen again.

They're not wasting any time out front, you think.

You lock eyes with Chef. He raises an eyebrow, glowers all the way into you.

"Sorry I'm late, Chef," you say, sheepishly. "It won't happen again."

He plucks the ticket from the printer. You tilt your head and wait for the call.

"Order fire," he says. "Four-top: two duck eggs, one eggs lamb, one pain perdu."

"*Oui,* Chef," you say.

Pans hammer down. Fat splashes into them.

You slug your Pedialyte and force back the nausea.

Hopefully Stefan will be here to jump in for you soon. Today it's your turn to hide out rolling pasta.

The printers begin buzzing again.

Another order spits out. And another, impatiently, behind it.

All you can do is put your head down and cook.

This sucks, you think. *Fuck brunch.*

But you *do* do it well when you do it.

SELECTED KITCHEN TERMINOLOGY

à la carte (of a menu or restaurant) listing or serving food that can be ordered as separate items, rather than part of a set meal; (of food) available on such a menu as separately priced items, not as part of a set meal

à la minute (of food) made to order; (of the cooking process) at the last minute

à sec (of liquid) heavily reduced to a syrupy consistency

accoutrements additional items served alongside the central component of a dish

acid a seasoning agent used to accentuate flavor, esp. citrus juice or vinegar

agnolotti a kind of ravioli typical of the Piedmont region of Italy, made with small pieces of flattened pasta dough, folded over any variety of fillings

aioli mayonnaise flavored with garlic

all day (of a particular food item) the total quantity that has been ordered by patrons or that remains to be prepared

amuse-bouche a bite-size hors d'oeuvre of the chef's choosing given to a patron at the top of a meal, free of charge, in order to give the guest a glimpse of what is to come

argan oil a nutty, aromatic culinary oil expressed from the seeds of the argan tree, native to southwestern Morocco, used for cooking, seasoning, dressing, and finishing

aromatics those ingredients that impart lively flavor or fragrance outside the normal range of lingual taste (which is limited to the flavors sweet, sour, salt, bitter, umami), chiefly alliums (e.g. garlic, onion, leek), hard-stemmed herbs (e.g. thyme, rosemary, bay), and spices (e.g. coriander seed, cinnamon bark, cardamom pod)

arroser to baste a given food product (usually with melted fat and aromatics) during stovetop cooking in order to accelerate the cooking process and/or enhance flavor

atelier a workshop or studio, esp. one used by an artist or designer

back waiter an FOH staff member who delivers food from the kitchen to the dining room, clears plates between courses, fills water glasses, and assists the chef de rang

bain-marie a container holding hot water into which a pan is placed for slow cooking or keeping warm; a double boiler (owing to the vessel's cylindrical shape, bains-marie are frequently used as storage containers for smallwares)

bar mop a heavy cotton towel used for cleaning work surfaces and to prevent burns while handling hot pots and pans in the kitchen

BEO (Banquet Event Order) any documentation detailing the requests of a large party reservation or private dining client

beurre blanc a semi-stable emulsion of reduced white wine and butter, usually flavored with shallots and vinegar or lemon juice, often accompanying seafood

bistro a small restaurant serving simple, moderately priced meals in a modest setting

BOH (Back of the House) the kitchen; also, the kitchen staff

Bonnet stove a custom-made cooking suite made by the French equipment manufacturer Bonnet, often held to be the top of the line

boquerones mild white anchovies marinated in vinegar and olive oil with garlic and parsley; a common Spanish tapa

bottarga the dried, pressed roe of a fish, usually either tuna (bottarga di tonno) or mullet (bottarga di muggine), that is produced and sold in blocks, which can be shaved or grated into various dishes

boudin blanc a pork-based "pudding"-style sausage common in French, Belgian, and Cajun cuisine, which typically contains liver, heart, milk, and sometimes eggs and other ingredients

bouillon the strained liquid that results from slowly simmering ingredients in water (in practice, bouillon differs from stock in that it is usually seasoned and reduced to a slightly more viscous consistency)

braise to sear (food) lightly and then stew slowly in a closed container until tender

brigade de cuisine the quasimilitary kitchen hierarchy delineated by Georges Auguste Escoffier in his c. 1903 opus *Le Guide Culinaire*

Brinata a white soft-rind sheep's milk cheese from Tuscany (aged twenty days)

brunoise (in knife work) a perfectly cubical vegetable dice of a size no greater than 3 × 3 × 3 mm

C-fold towel A rectangular leaf of paper toweling that has been folded twice lengthwise so that a cross-section resembles the letter C

Cambro a brand of kitchen equipment (CAMBRO®) whose name has been adopted in common vernacular to denote any of several storage containers made by said company, most commonly the Cam-Squares® line, available in 2, 4, 6, 8, 12, 18, and 22 quart capacities, or the Cam-wear® hotel style food pan line; "pass the stock through a chinois into a 22-quart Cambro"; "put all your mise en place into ninth Cambros"

cake tester a steel pin one inserts into and removes from a given food product to assess its doneness (based on any residue or residual heat the pin carries with it when removed)

canapé a small piece of bread or pastry with a savory topping, often served with drinks at a reception or formal party; in the common vernacular, "canapé" is used interchangeably, if erroneously, with "amuse-bouche" and "hors d'oeuvre"

caramelization the process by which the sugar molecules in a given food product (either native or supplementary) are heated to the point at which they relinquish their water content (roughly 340°F) and proceed to fragment into the isomers and polymers responsible for the characteristic caramel flavor and color; the noticeable results of this process (the term "caramelization" is often mistakenly used to refer to the Maillard reaction)

cartouche a disc of parchment paper with a hole in the center meant to retard the evaporation of moisture from a pan of cooking food without generating the same level of condensation that a conventional lid would

cassoulet a bean stew usually made with bacon or other meat

caul fat (usually of a pig) the amniotic membrane enclosing a fetus; the lining of a pig's stomach

cazuela a shallow round earthenware cooking vessel

cervelle de veau veal brains

chanterelle (*Cantharellus cibarius*) an edible woodland mushroom with a yellow funnel-shaped cap and a faint aroma of apricots, found in both Eurasia and North America

charcuterie cooked or cured meats that are served cold, e.g. terrines, rillettes, pâtés, galatines, boudins, hams, confits, etc.

Château-Chalon a nutty, AOC (Appellation d'Origine Contrôlée) vin jaune made from the Savagnin grape varietal in the Jura wine region of France near the village of Château-Chalon; also, a sauce made from wine of this sort (Château-Chalon is a traditional accompaniment for *poulet de Bresse,* a breed of chicken originating in the nearby Bresse area)

chef (usually executive chef) a highly skilled professional cook who has expertise in every area of the kitchen; the chief cook in a given restaurant or hotel

chef de cuisine (often in a restaurant that is part of a larger group of restaurants owned by the same person or persons) a chef who runs a particular kitchen or branch of a given restaurant group in the stead of an executive chef; usually the executive chef's is still the primary name associated with the restaurant, but the chef de cuisine runs the operation day to day (e.g. Chef Thomas Keller's restaurant Per Se is currently helmed by chef de cuisine Eli Kaimeh)

chef de partie the cook responsible for governing a particular area of production in a kitchen, e.g. fish or meat; usually a chef de partie manages several other cooks below him or her on that station

chef(s) de rang the chief liaison(s) between the kitchen and the front of the house (in a large restaurant, the dining room is broken into sections called *rangs;* the chef de rang is the person responsible to the kitchen for each of those sections)

chef plongeur head dishwasher

chine (as noun) the backbone of an animal, or a cut of meat containing this bone; (as verb) to remove this bone from said cut of meat

chinois a conical sieve with an extremely fine mesh, used to strain custards, purees, soups, and sauces, producing a very smooth texture

chit a short official note, memorandum, or voucher, typically recording a sum owed

circulator *see* thermal immersion circulator

collagen the main structural ingredient of animal connective tissue, which yields gelatin when boiled

combi an oven capable of producing a combination of steam heat and dry heat, prized for allowing users to precisely control the humidity of the air inside the cooking chamber

commis a junior cook employed by a restaurant (unlike a stagiaire, a commis works for pay, though their tasks are usually similar)

compression the process of vacuum-sealing ingredients (usually fruits and vegetables) in plastic in such a way that their cell structure is compressed in order to concentrate color and flavor (compression projects often involve the simultaneous infusion of an additional flavor, e.g. a spice, liquid, or fat, as the vacuum process forces the flavor into the item being compressed)

confit (as verb) to preserve, often in fat; (as noun) the product of this process

convection oven an oven that circulates the air around its chamber, usually with a fan

cook (as verb) to physically denature (food) by the administration of heat; (as noun) a person employed by a restaurant to do such work (cooks are those who have not yet graduated to the level of chef; while all chefs are cooks, not all cooks are chefs)

cornichon a pickled gherkin cucumber, usually of a dill flavor profile

cover an individual guest, often as part of a tally of guests: "we did seventy-six covers at lunch today"

croquette a small rod or orb of chopped vegetables, meat, or fish coated in bread crumbs and often fried

crosne a sweet root vegetable similar to the Jerusalem artichoke, distinguished by its grublike appearance

Cryovac brand name of a vacuum-sealing company, which has been adopted in the common vernacular to refer to any reduced oxygen packaging (ROP) process or apparatus

cuisine a style or method of cooking, esp. as characteristic of a particular country, region, or establishment

cuisson the method of cooking something; also, the results of said method

deli a round plastic vessel with an 8-to-64-ounce capacity, similar to the containers in which one receives prepared goods from the deli (these are also often referred to as quart or pint containers)

demi-glace a jus (typically veal or beef) that has been reinforced (i.e. cooked again) with wine, vegetables, and meat trim and reduced to a shiny sauce consistency

dice (as verb) to cut a given food product into cubes; (as noun) the resulting cubes

drop tray a rectangular tray made of thin-gauge steel upon which prepared food items are placed, or dropped, throughout service; drop trays can be used for seasoning, retherming, and presenting to Chef

dupe pad a pad of paper on which waitstaff write down orders from guests; the paper is often backed with carbon so that a duplicate of the order can be given to another (usually the kitchen) if necessary

emulsion a colloidal suspension of one liquid in another with which it is typically immiscible

en crépinette (of meat) wrapped in caul fat

enokitake a Japanese mushroom used for soups and salads (the cultivated enoki, aka straw mushroom, is remarkably different in appearance and flavor from its wild kin, *Flammulina velutipes,* which is pink in color with a larger cap and a stouter stem

entremetier a vegetable cook

evasée a saucepan whose circumference at its top is greater than that at its base, used primarily for evaporating liquids

extern a cook working in but not an official employee of a given restaurant; professional externships are required of most culinary school students

fabrication (in butchery) the reduction of a whole animal to smaller pieces

farce (in food) a filling of any sort

fat any natural oily or greasy substance, usually derived from animal bodies or plant products, that is used in cooking

fermentation the chemical breakdown of a substance by bacteria, yeasts, or other microorganisms, typically involving effervescence and the giving off of heat; the process of this kind involved in the making of beer, wine, and liquor, in which sugars are converted to ethyl alcohol

ficelle (French for "thread") a small, very thin loaf of French bread

filbert a cultivated hazel tree that bears edible oval nuts; also, a nut from such a tree

fines herbs (pl.) a mélange of fresh chopped herbs, esp. parsley, chives, tarragon, and chervil

fingerling a variety of potato having a pink, yellow, blue, or light tan skin and flesh, so named for its similarity in size and shape to a human finger

finnan haddie haddock cured with the smoke of green wood, turf, or peat

fire to begin preparing a given food item

flat-top a stovetop cooking surface made of cast iron or black steel that shields pans from open flame while still conducting the same amount of heat; flat-tops are preferred to conventional open burners because they help prevent inadvertent in-pan flare-ups and because they can accommodate many pans at once

floor the dining room; also, the staff of the dining room

fluid gel a relatively stable colloidal suspension of a solid dispersed in a liquid, which bears properties of both states of matter; typically fluid gels are chilled 1 percent pectin solutions that have been pureed into a more liquid form

FOH (Front of the House) the dining room; also, the dining room staff

foie gras a food product made of the liver of a duck or goose that has been specially fattened; by French law, foie gras is defined as the liver of a duck fattened by force-feeding corn with a gavage tube, although outside France it is occasionally produced using natural feeding

fondue a thick sauce usually containing emulsified dairy

food service film industry nomenclature for plastic wrap or cling film

forceps pincers or tweezers, usually of surgical origin, that assist in handling food delicately, especially as compared to the more conventional tongs; often called metal fingers

gambas Spanish term for prawns

Garasuki a heavyweight Japanese knife designed for butchering large birds and small land animals

garde manger a cool, well-ventilated area of the kitchen where cold items such as salads are prepared; also, the person who works this section of the kitchen

garnish any item that decorates or accompanies the central component of a given dish

gavage the administration of food or drugs by force, esp. to an animal, typically through a tube leading down the throat to the stomach

gelatin a virtually colorless and tasteless substance derived from collagen, the introduction of which allows a liquid to take on the properties of a solid at room temperature

girolle the French term for *chanterelle*

glace (as noun) a sauce that has been reduced to a thick, shiny consistency; (as verb, glacé) to coat a foodstuff with such a sauce

Griswold brand name of a now-defunct maker of iron cookware that has been adopted in the common vernacular to refer to cast-iron or black steel pans

guanciale unsmoked Umbrian salumi made from salted and spiced pig jowl

Gyutou a general-purpose Japanese chef knife with a wide blade ranging from eight to twelve inches in length

HACCP (Hazard Analysis and Critical Control Points) a food safety program in which a victualer tracks the entire life span (receipt, storage, preparation, service, etc.) of a given product in order to identify all points at which said product may be subject to bacterial contamination or proliferation; in the state of New York, approved HACCP programs are mandatory for any victualer wishing to practice ROP

half pan *see* hotel pan

hanger steak a small flap of belly-side cow meat, known for an intense beef flavor, said to hang from the cow's diaphragm; also known as butcher's steak, as it is the most flavorful cut, which butchers would often keep for themselves

hollandaise a creamy emulsion of egg yolks and clarified butter often seasoned with salt, acid, and mustard; one of the five mother sauces, from which all other sauces are said to derive

Honesuki a triangular Japanese poultry boning knife

hood an exhaust system positioned above cooking apparatuses, which sucks hot air, steam, and smoke out of the kitchen

hors d'oeuvre a small savory dish served in advance of a meal

hotel pan (third/sixth/ninth/half) a vessel of thin-gauge stainless steel, which, owing to the metal's conductivity, is ideal for storing prepared food at a particular temperature, either warm or hot depending on the application; most refrigeration units, hot tables, chafing racks, and shelves are designed around the standard dimensions of the variously sized hotel pans

houndstooth pants (pl.) black-and-white-checked pants considered standard attire for professional cooks, preferred because of the pattern's ability to conceal stains; while houndstooth checks are standard for cooks, most chefs work in black trousers

induction burner any stove system that heats cooking vessels by way of electromagnetic induction, as opposed to the heat transfer method of open flame or heat coil cooking. Induction burners are sometimes preferred because they are energy efficient and because of their ability to heat a cooking vessel to a more controlled temperature, though gas ranges are considered much sexier; the major drawback to induction is that the cooking vessel must be ferromagnetic, i.e. iron or stainless steel, as induction burners will not work on aluminum (this, however, is only a minor drawback, because virtually nobody in serious kitchens uses aluminum cookware)

jackfruit the large edible fruit of the tropical tree *Artocarpus heterophyllus,* common in Indian and Southeast Asian cuisine; the ripe fruit is quite sweet, often used in desserts, whereas the unripe fruit, usually braised or stewed, is often used by vegetarians as a substitute for meat in Thai cooking

jus a stock or bouillon that has been reduced to sauce consistency

knife kit a cook's collection of work tools including knives and other instruments

Kumamoto (*Crassostrea sikamea*) a small Japanese oyster characterized by a deep, almost bowl-shaped shell festooned with flutes, knobs, and points; owing to their slow growth rate and remarkable sweetness, Kumamotos are highly prized, often fetching high prices and warranting strict rules of nomenclature

legume any plant of the pea family (*Leguminosae*); also, the fruit or seed of such a plant

Lexan a transparent plastic (polycarbonate) of high impact strength, originally used for cockpit canopies, bulletproof screens, etc., adopted as a suitable material for food storage containers because of its durability; also, a container made of this material

line the part of a professional kitchen where food is prepared during service

liquor liquid in which something has been steeped or cooked; liquid that drains from food during cooking; *see also* cuisson

LOI (Last Order In) in a state of service when all guest orders have been delivered to the kitchen: "Is that it for the night, Chef?" "Yes, we are LOI."

lowboy a long, squat refrigeration unit, approximately three feet in height, which doubles as a tabletop surface

lychee a small rounded fruit with sweet white scented flesh, a large central stone, and a thin rough skin (also called lychee nut when dried); also, the Chinese tree that bears this fruit (*Nephelium litchi*)

mafalde a fringed, ribbon-shaped pasta that can be described as some midpoint between fettuccini and lasagna sheets

Maillard reaction a form of nonenzymatic browning, resulting from a chemical reaction between an amino acid and a reducing sugar, usually requiring heat and often yielding hundreds of different flavor and aroma compounds; the process differs from caramelization in that it requires the presence of amino acids (examples of the Maillard reaction include the coloration of toasted bread, fried potatoes, and roasted meats)

mandoline a device consisting of a flat frame with adjustable cutting blades for slicing vegetables

marbled (adj., of meat) marked by a noticeable lacework of fat; since fat imparts flavor, the more marbled a piece of meat, the better

meal period a shift of service, e.g. breakfast, lunch, brunch, dinner, or late night

meat glue *see* transglutaminase

Metro rack brand name of a type of wire shelving, which has been adopted in the common vernacular to describe any shelving of this sort

Michelin Guide (*Le Guide Michelin,* specifically the red book) a French hotel and restaurant guidebook that reviews and rates restaurants on a three-star scale; Michelin stars are the most coveted honor in the global restaurant arena, often the source of culinary nervous breakdowns and mania

Microplane brand name of a fine metal grater used to zest citrus fruits, or to shave hard cheeses, spices, truffles, or other such items over food, which has been adopted in the common vernacular to describe any grater of this sort

mise en place the activity of preparing and collecting ingredients in advance of service; also, the items produced by this activity

mousse any preparation that incorporates air bubbles to give it a light, frothy texture

MR/M/MW (of doneness) medium rare, i.e. having an internal temperature of approximately 130°–135°F; medium, i.e. having an internal temperature of approximately 140°–145°F; medium well, i.e. having an internal temperature of approximately 150°–155°F

noisette d'agneau a small round piece of lamb meat

ninth pan *see* hotel pan

oui French for "yes"

oven an enclosed insulated chamber in which ambient heat (i.e. hot air) is used to cook food; *compare* stove

Pakkawood a solid material consisting of layered hardwood veneers that have been impregnated with phenolic thermosetting resins to prevent moisture retention; Pakkawood is ideal for knife handles as it has the desirable look and feel of wood and the durability and hygienic properties of synthetic materials

par the expected or necessary quantity of a given foodstuff kept or prepared regularly in a kitchen

paring knife a small knife used mainly for peeling fruits and vegetables

pass (as noun) the area of the kitchen where food is plated or finalized and transferred to the custody of the waitstaff; (as verb) to press or strain through a fine strainer or sieve

patina a gray gloss or sheen that develops on a high-carbon knife, produced by age and polishing

pavé a rectilinear cut of meat or fish, so named because its size and shape resemble a paving stone

Pedro Ximenez a white grape grown in certain regions of Spain, used to make a dark, rich sherry wine of the same name; a sweet vinegar produced from such a sherry, often aged in oak casks to a syrupy consistency

Peltex a slotted metal spatula designed for turning fish, the name of which is borrowed from Nogent Peltex, a brand name line of such spatulas

Petty a small, thin knife of five to six inches designed for small detail work

piano the surface area of the stove anterior to the heating surface, so named for its resemblance in size and shape to the keyboard of a piano; pans and drop trays are often placed on the piano to keep their contents warm without delivering direct heat to the food

Piave an Italian cow's milk cheese from the Piave River valley; depending on its age, the color ranges from off-white to yellow, and the mouth feel ranges from mild and bouncy like a young Pecorino to hard and pungent like Parmigiano Reggiano

pickup a group of guest orders to be prepared simultaneously; the act of preparing such a group

pimentón dulce sweet smoked paprika from Spain

piquillo a small, sweet red chili (with a negligible ranking on the Scoville scale), native to northern Spain

plancha a steel plate (usually attached to the stove as part of a cooking suite) on which food is seared directly

plat du jour a special of the day

pluche a sprig or leaf of a given herb

PPX (*personne particulièrement extraordinaire*) an important guest, a VIP

poissonnier a fish cook

pommes fondant a dish of potatoes cooked in stock (usually animal-based) and butter

pommes purees smooth mashed potatoes

pope's nose the fatty piece of meat on a chicken rump that holds the tail feathers

POS (Point of Sale) the computing system through which an FOH staff member distributes relevant information regarding guest requests to necessary parties (e.g. kitchen and bar), from which guest checks and receipts are produced, and in which financial records and business figures are stored and calculated

prawn a marine crustacean (Leander and other genera, class Malacostraca) that resembles a large shrimp

prep (as noun) the work that is done in advance of service; (as verb) to engage in such work

primal (in butchery) of the initial group of sections, cuts, or quarters separated by the butcher in meat fabrication

proofing box a chamber or cabinet, sometimes heated by an outside power source, designed to store bread doughs while yeast activates; proofing boxes are also often used to house prepared foods meant to be kept warm throughout catering services, and for large format dehydration projects, such as tomato confit

puree the smooth, creamy substance made when a solid is liquidized mechanically

push an especially busy duration of time throughout service or prep

quenelle (as noun) an oblong, rounded, or three-sided scoop of food, usually a puree, resembling a football; (as verb) to create such a shape with a spoon

range a cooking apparatus consisting of one or more oven (q.v.) components and one or more stove (q.v.) components

ramp a wild onion native to the Appalachian region of the United States known for a mild yet robust flavor

reduce to increase the viscosity of a liquid by the administration of heat

rethermalize to reintroduce heat after an initial cooking process

risotto an Italian dish of rice (usually arborio) cooked slowly with stock and butter

roast (as verb) to cook slowly using ambient heat, as in an oven; (as noun) any food prepared in this way

roe the mass of eggs contained in the ovaries of a fish

rocket alternative name for arugula, a peppery Mediterranean leaf plant of the cabbage family eaten raw or wilted

romesco a Catalonian sauce made from nuts and red peppers; there are myriad recipes for romesco containing any or all of the following ingredients: pine nuts, hazelnuts, almonds (chiefly Marconas), piquillo peppers, roasted tomato, raw garlic, roasted garlic, parsley leaves, chili flake, sherry vinegar, bread crust, egg, anchovy, and chocolate

rondeau a wide, round, shallow sautoir with handles on each side, used for a variety of techniques such as reducing sauces, making risottos, braising meats, and searing large quantities of food at once

ROP (Reduced Oxygen Packaging) the process of sealing (product) in a plastic vessel from which air is removed via vacuum; ROP is a fundamental step in sous vide cookery

rôtisseur a cook who works the roast (meat) station

roulade a dish cooked or served in the form of a roll, typically made from a flat piece of meat, fish, or sponge cake spread with a soft filling and rolled up into a spiral

RTG (Ready to Go) alternative term for "there"

salamander (colloquial) a broiler-style cooking apparatus that delivers heat from above by way of an open flame

salsa verde a pesto-style sauce made with any of the broad-leafed soft herbs (e.g. parsley, cilantro, tarragon, basil, chervil, chive, etc.) blended with any or all of the following ingredients: olive oil, garlic, salt, acid, egg, anchovy, pickled vegetables

salumi meats that have been salted, smoked, dried, or otherwise cured and flavored, which are then sliced and served in advance of a meal

sapori forte any sauce in which a series of bold components work in harmony together, in effect canceling each other's relative strengths

sauce any liquid served with food to add moisture or flavor

sauce consistency the viscosity a liquid must reach before being served, which varies from case to case based on what the particular sauce or the particular dish calls for; it is usually judged by the way the liquid behaves on the back of a spoon or its relative tackiness when rubbed between two fingers

sauce rôti any sauce made from a stock of roasted bones or vegetables

sauté to fry atop the stove very quickly in shallow oil

sauteuse a shallow frying pan with angled sides, so named because it is more feminine in form than a sautoir

sautoir a shallow frying pan with vertical sides, so named because it is more masculine in form than a sauteuse

Scamorza a mild white Italian cheese made originally from buffalo's milk, but now chiefly from cow's milk, typically produced in a pear shape

Scoville scale a measuring system that grades the pungency or "spiciness" of peppers

sear to burn or scorch the surface of something with sudden, direct, intense heat

season to add a quality or feature (e.g. salt, spice, acid) to (food) so as to enhance its naturally occurring flavors or to contribute new ones

service (in restaurants) the period of time

during which the restaurant is open for business and actively preparing food for patrons

Sicilian pistachio the sweet green seed from a tree of the same name, which differs from the traditional pistachio in softness of texture, vibrancy of color, and richness of flavor

sieve a utensil consisting of a wire or plastic mesh held in a frame, used for straining solids from liquids, for separating coarser from finer particles, or for reducing soft solids to a pulp

skate a typically large marine fish of the ray family (Rajidae) with a cartilaginous skeleton and a flattened diamond-shaped body; the flesh of such a fish

slurry a semiliquid mixture of fine particles suspended in water

smallwares those cooking utensils that are portable (e.g. part of a knife kit) or have no fixed location within the kitchen (e.g. a hand blender)

sofrito a sauce base of vegetables (often including carrot, celery, onion, garlic, pepper, and tomato) that have been finely diced and caramelized in olive oil

SOP (Standard Operating Procedure) the way things are done, particularly from a managerial perspective, in business; a recipe for how situations are handled

soubise a white sauce made from pureed onions that have been gently sweated until soft

soufflé a dish caused to rise as by the addition of heat or air

sous chef a restaurant's second in command

sous vide (as noun) a cooking technique in which the item to be cooked is vacuum-sealed and (usually) submerged in a thermo-regulated liquid wherein it is brought to a highly specific internal temperature; (as verb) to prepare food using this technique; (as adj.) (of a food) having been cooked this way

soya oil an oil pressed from *Glycine max,* the Asian soybean, prized in cooking for its high flash point and neutral flavor

spoon water a vessel of water (usually a small bain-marie) for storing and rinsing spoons and other cooking utensils throughout service; according to health department regulations, utensils intended for frequent reuse must be stored in constantly running water (e.g. Dipwell containers) or washed between uses, though most restaurants violate this regulation in favor of a spoon water basin that is changed out regularly

sprezzatura an easy facility in accomplishing difficult actions that hides the conscious effort that went into them

stagiaire a transient member of a kitchen staff who works without pay, voluntarily, in order that he or she might learn techniques and practices unique to said kitchen; an intern

steam kettle a kettle- or pot-shaped cooking apparatus enclosed in an outer wall, or jacket; it introduces heat to its contents (usually liquid) by channeling steam into the void between the cooking surface and the jacket, which optimizes heat distribution and promotes even cooking

stew to cook slowly in liquid; any dish preparation of this sort

steward a custodian employed to clean the entire restaurant, usually after closing, typically overnight

stock the strained liquid that results from slowly simmering ingredients (chiefly animal bones or vegetables) in water

stove an unenclosed surface that uses direct heat (typically flame or electricity) to heat a vessel in which food is cooked; *compare* oven

squab a young unfledged pigeon; also, the flesh of such a bird as food

sub-primal (in butchery) secondary to or

smaller than primal cuts

sugo a thick sauce or gravy, usually incorporating sofrito, tomato, and meat juices

suite a single unit of kitchen equipment (usually custom-built) containing multiple cooking apparatuses (e.g. ovens, salamanders, and a variety of individually controlled stove surfaces) for use by several people at once

Sujihiki a long, thin Japanese knife used for slicing meat and fish

sweat to draw the moisture out of a given food product (usually a vegetable) by cooking it gently in a pan until soft, at a temperature low enough to preclude caramelization and/or the Maillard reaction

Taleggio a washed-rind cow's milk cheese from Lombardy known for a pungent odor yet mild, salty flavor

tamis a kitchen utensil shaped somewhat like a snare drum with a cylindrical edge made of metal or wood that supports a disc of fine metal, nylon, or horsehair mesh that acts as a strainer, grater, or food mill through which food is pushed or scraped

tartare a dish in which the central component (usually meat or seafood) is finely chopped, seasoned, and served raw

temper to slowly introduce (food) to heat or

warmth without actually cooking: "to avoid scrambling the custard, you must first temper the eggs by slowly drizzling in the hot milk, whisking constantly"

terrine a meat, seafood, or vegetable mixture that has been cooked or otherwise prepared in advance and allowed to cool or set in its container, typically served in slices; a container used for such a dish, typically of an oblong shape and made of earthenware

there (colloquial) in a state of complete readiness

thermal immersion circulator an electrically powered device that circulates and heats a warm fluid kept at a precise and stable temperature, used to maintain accuracy and control sous vide cookery

third pan *see* hotel pan

tilt skillet a large, vertically walled, plancha-like piece of cooking equipment used to sear and braise foods, uniquely outfitted with a gear and crank system that allows its user to angle the surface of the apparatus, so as to remove its contents more quickly

toast point a toasted bias-cut piece of bread (usually baguette) on which various toppings can be placed or spread

Tokyo turnip the root vegetable of a young

turnip plant, preferred to its full-grown kin for its tender flavor and attractive size and shape

tortuga (colloquial) Spanish for "tortoise"; any person or thing that is exceptionally slow-moving

trail (as verb) to audition for a position in a kitchen by way of working a station for a night (for free), "trailing" the work of the cook currently employed there; (as noun) one who performs or the occasion of performing such an audition

transglutaminase an enzyme that catalyzes the formation of a thermo-irreversible covalent bond between a free amine group (e.g. protein- or peptide-bound lysine) and the gamma-carboxamide group of protein- or peptide-bound glutamine; aka meat glue

trattoria a small restaurant serving simple food, often for takeout

trim any usable material that results from, but will not be used in, a given prep project; a more refined term for scraps, leftovers

turn (as noun) a stretch of business wherein every seat in the dining room is filled once; busy restaurants do multiple turns per meal period; (as verb) to shape a vegetable with a paring knife in such a way that it takes a rounded, football-like shape, traditionally with seven equal sides

uni the gonad of a sea urchin (male or female), prized for its buttery texture and strong sea flavor

verjus a highly acidic juice made by pressing unripe grapes, crabapples, or other sour fruit

violet mustard a condiment from the Brive-la-Gaillarde region of France, made with grape must, mustard seeds, wine, vinegar, salt, and spices. Its flavor is sweeter and milder than that of conventional Dijon

waitstaff FOH employees who take orders from customers, communicate them to the kitchen, and serve the resultant food

walk-in box the large cold storage facility in a restaurant, which can be walked into

water bath in sous vide cookery, the temperature-regulated pool in which food is cooked and/or rethermalized

whites (colloquial) the standard work attire for cooks and chefs, consisting primarily of coat, pants, and apron

wine key the most common term for a corkscrew wine opener in the restaurant industry

Wondra flour brand name of a finely ground flour ideal for making roux and dredging items to be fried because of its anti-clumping properties, which has been adopted in the common vernacular to refer to any flour of this sort

xanthan gum a polysaccharide secreted by the plant-based bacterium *Xanthomonas campestris* during fermentation, which, when isolated, is used as a food additive to increase a liquid's viscosity and promote emulsion

Y peeler a vegetable peeler in the shape of the letter Y, whose peeling edge spans the gap between the two arms

Yo-Deba a heavy Japanese knife used in animal butchery for cutting through bones

zest (as verb) to remove the essential-oil-rich skin (of a citrus fruit) without cutting into the rind; (as noun) the product of this process

Z report the financial report issued by a POS system when all sales on a given day or meal period are finalized

ACKNOWLEDGMENTS

It would be easy for me to go on at length thanking the many people who have contributed to the production of this book. There is my agent, Kris, my professional teammate, whose faith in me is the reason this story isn't buried on a flash drive somewhere in Brooklyn right now. The support she has shown me since the day I met her is something I'll treasure until I'm gray and stooped. There is my editor, Pamela, without whose guidance and motivation I might still be trying to figure out my first revisions. Firmly but gently, she has ushered me through this quite foreign and often onerous publication process with a grace and patience I daresay only she possesses. There are the tremendous production and design teams at Ballantine/Random House, whose collective energy in creating a fabulous package for this book is something I stand humbly beside in awe. And then there are all the friends and family and classmates and college professors whose encouragement throughout the years has allowed me to believe that I not only have a story worth telling, but that I also have the equipment to tell it right. I could consume reams of paper expressing my gratitude for these folks.

But what I'd really like to use this space for is to acknowledge the ones who initially lit the pilot — that mighty population of cooks and chefs for whom this book is a daily reality. They are my inspiration. Their dedication to feeding others is what gets me out of bed in the morning, and the example they set for us every day is what keeps me going into the night. Of this great lot, dearest to me of course are the ones I've been fortunate enough to see in action; the ones I've had the opportunity to work with, work for, stand beside, or otherwise help out in that sacred space around the stove; and the ones whose work, in one way or another, continues to inform my own. They are, in regretfully incomplete form: Duce Inthalassy, Gary Moran, Johannes Sanzin, Sean Gray, Steven Davis, Brian Young, Rory O'Farrell, Joe Barraco, Johnny Lewis, Calvert Rose, Wolfgang Stoiber, Jason Neroni, Nick Grosz, Alex Sze, Jaime Young, Matthew Burdi, Marcello De Andrade, Julie Farias, Nicholas Morgenstern, Warren Baird, Gabriel Cruz, Steve Peterson, Brad McDonald, Jonathan Black, Greg Kuzia-Carmel, Chloé Lasseron, Monique Bourgea, Kelly White, Stephen Hernandez, Jonathan Park, Morgan Schofield, Giles Clark, Jordan Kahn, Will Aghajanian, Francis Derby, Mathias Dahlgren, Alex Stupak, Michael Coté, and Isabel Coss. And of course, my most cherished friend and favorite person to cook beside, Michelle Nicole Merlo.

It is because of all these remarkable people, and many others like them, that I was able to write this book.

ABOUT THE AUTHOR

Michael Gibney began working in restaurants at the age of sixteen and assumed his first sous chef position at twenty-two. He ascended to executive sous chef while at Tavern on the Green, where he managed an eighty-person staff. He's worked in the kitchens of Morgans Hotel Group, 10 Downing in Manhattan, and Governor in Brooklyn's DUMBO, among many others. Over the course of his career, he has had the opportunity to work alongside cooks and chefs from many of the nation's best restaurants, including Alinea, Per Se, Eleven Madison Park, Daniel, Jean-Georges, Le Bernardin, Bouley, Ducasse, Corton, wd~50, and Momofuku. In addition to his experience in the food service industry, Gibney also holds a BFA in painting from Pratt Institute and an MFA in nonfiction writing from Columbia University. He lives in Brooklyn.

The employees of Thorndike Press hope you have enjoyed this Large Print book. All our Thorndike, Wheeler, and Kennebec Large Print titles are designed for easy reading, and all our books are made to last. Other Thorndike Press Large Print books are available at your library, through selected bookstores, or directly from us.

For information about titles, please call:
(800) 223-1244

or visit our Web site at:
http://gale.cengage.com/thorndike

To share your comments, please write:
Publisher
Thorndike Press
10 Water St., Suite 310
Waterville, ME 04901